Fact or Fiction?
Jesus According To The Evidence

Dan Stephenson

Focus Infinity

Toronto Los Angeles

FOCUS
infinity

Fact or Fiction
Jesus: According to Evidence
Copyright © 2017 by Dan Stephenson

Library of Congress Control Number
2016962927

All rights are reserved. No part of this publication may be reproduced, stored in a retrieval system or transmitted in any form or by any means, electronic, mechanical, photocopying, recording or otherwise, without prior permission of the Publisher.

Focus Infinity
Toronto. Los Angeles
www.focusinfinity.com

All Scripture quotations, unless otherwise indicated, are taken from the Holy Bible, New International Version®, NIV®. Copyright ©1973, 1978, 1984, 2011 by Biblica, Inc.™ Used by permission of Zondervan. All rights reserved worldwide. www.zondervan.com The "NIV" and "New International Version" are trademarks registered in the United States Patent and Trademark Office by Biblica, Inc.™

For Tracey

Contents

About the Author vii
1. My Love Affair With Evidence 1
2. What Is Evidence? 5
3. The Bible and Other Types of Evidence 11
4. Voir Dire: God and Miracles 19
5. Is Jesus Real? 33
6. The Birth of Jesus 39
7. The Life of Jesus 45
8. The Death of Jesus 59
9. The Resurrection of Jesus 65
10. Experiential Evidence 93
11. "Why?" – Questions Behind the Evidence 99
12. Does It Hold Water? 109
13. What Smart People Do With Evidence 113
Resources for Further Study 123
Acknowledgements 125
Notes 129

ABOUT THE AUTHOR

Dan Stephenson grew up in Ann Arbor, Michigan. He attended college at UCLA, where he was an All-American swimmer. After receiving his engineering degree from UCLA, he went to law school at the University of Michigan, and practiced law in Michigan for 27 years after graduating. He now practices law in California and North Carolina, the states where his children (2) and grandchildren (4) reside. He is admitted to practice law in Michigan, California and North Carolina. In his 34 years of law practice, Dan has tried many high-profile cases, including the jury trial involving the crash of Northwest Airlines Flight 255. At the time, the crash was the second-worst in the nation's history, and the trial lasted 18 months. Dan's cases have involved complex science and technology, from aerospace to brain surgery. He has received accolades as a lawyer, such as "Litigation Star" (Benchmark), "Best Lawyers in America," "Preeminent" (Martindale-Hubbell), and "Super Lawyer" (Law & Politics). Dan would be the first to tell you that these descriptors are mere puffery and not "evidence" of his legal prowess.

Dan has authored legal treatises, including a chapter on expert witness cross-examination in *From the Trenches: Strategies and Tips From 21 of the Nation's Top Trial Lawyers*. He is also a published novelist. His first novel, *The Underwater Window*, set in the fast-paced world of Olympic swimming, was highly acclaimed. In his swimming career, Dan has set ten world records (two of which still stand in 2017) and won 17 world championships in masters competition.

DAN STEPHENSON

Dan serves on the boards of Focus Infinity, a multicultural outreach ministry, and ZimZam Global, a leadership training and church planting ministry in Africa and south Asia. He previously chaired the board of Michigan Theological Seminary. He has taken classes toward a Masters degree at Dallas Theological Seminary in his paltry spare time. Dan enjoys hanging out with his grandchildren, teaching Sunday School, hiking the bluffs at Malibu with his wife Tracey, playing a little golf from time to time, and cheering for Wolverines and Bruins, especially at the Rose Bowl.

1

MY LOVE AFFAIR WITH EVIDENCE

My name is Dan Stephenson and I am an evidence junkie. Evidence dominates my world. I am happiest when I have it, preferably in abundance. When I don't have it, my brain aches and I'm fidgety until I get it. If I had any spare change, I would use it to buy evidence.

Yes, I'm a lawyer. Lawyers are a breed apart. By that, I don't mean that we're above average – just different from normal people. We've been thoroughly studied by social scientists, and the one personality trait about lawyers that is most different from normal people is this: <u>skepticism</u>. On the "Caliper" scale for skepticism, lawyers are squarely in the 90th percentile.[1] Lawyers, of course, sternly doubt the studies. No one knows whether skeptical people gravitate toward the law or the profession drives us to skepticism. In either event, we can all agree that skeptics crave evidence.

I'm not just any kind of lawyer but a <u>courtroom</u> lawyer, the kind that goes to court and argues cases in front of judges and juries. Those are tough audiences. They like evidence too. They like <u>good</u> evidence. The side with the best evidence usually wins. Notice I didn't say "the most" evidence. Evidence can be strong or weak, and a case may turn on a single piece. But I'm getting ahead of myself.

I've been trying cases and arguing appeals for 34 years. Before that, I was in law school for three years. My father was a lawyer. So I've had a relationship (acquaintance, courtship, marriage) with the law for most of my life. Being a courtroom lawyer teaches you the value of evidence, where and how to dig for it, and what to do with it once you have it. It ingrains in you an evidence-based view of the world. Needless to say, that mindset is hard to shut off when you leave the courtroom. So, for example, my hobby is competitive swimming. I have a wealth of evidence about what makes a swimmer go fast. Some of that evidence is hard data – times, training sets, lactic acid levels, and heart rates. Some of it is experiential. When a new training theory comes out, I want to try it. I won't adopt it, however, until I've tried it myself and run my own personal data through the old brain computer.

I wasn't always a lawyer, of course. Before that, in college, I was a bit of a math-science geek who wore (*wore!*) a slide-rule on my hip. I studied mechanical engineering. Engineering takes theory to the practical level. You solve problems. You build things. Guess what you need in order to do that? Evidence.

It was when I was in college that I met Jesus. I grew up in wonderful family in the Midwestern US and went to church on occasion. Frankly, I found it pretty boring. I heard the name Jesus, but I didn't know if he was a real person or not. I heard he was a good man, a moral teacher. But that had no influence on me. His existence or non-existence was inconsequential to my life. I suspect that vast numbers of people in the US have this sort of non-relationship with Jesus.

When I got to college, I made new friends and among them were people who were markedly different. They didn't just talk about Jesus, they lived their lives like he was real. They didn't just go to boring church on Sundays, they worshiped and prayed and talked about Jesus every day. This was new to me, and my evidence wheels started spinning. I was curious and listened. I asked questions. When I was leaving school for the summer after my freshman year, one of my friends gave me a Bible to read and, to be polite, I promised I'd read it over the summer. Foolish promise! It's a massively large book! I started reading in the New Testament, and before long, it became clear that the Jesus in the Bible was different from what I'd heard. He was a good teacher, yes, but what was striking was how he spoke. He spoke with "authority" – his listeners heard it and I heard it myself. I resolved to gather the evidence. Forty years later, I have not stopped examining it.

The purpose of this book is to lay out the evidence about Jesus. Believe me, there's a lot. I've examined a mountain of evidence and read hundreds of books. Don't worry, though. I'm going to distill it for you and focus on the most important things. I'm going to speak in plain language, as I would to a jury. And I'm not going to push you into making any decisions or joining any groups. You will undoubtedly form some judgments along the way, and all I ask is that they be evidence-based.

In the pages below, we are going to examine several different kinds of evidence about Jesus. More has been written about Jesus than about anyone who ever lived. As you will see, there is evidence from history, science, archaeology, Biblical and non-Biblical literature, customs, and experiences. It runs the gamut from direct and tangible evidence to circumstantial, hearsay, and expert testimony. My contribution to the topic is to bring a reasoned and experienced analysis. I can help distinguish strong from weak evidence. Most important, we'll see if the pieces of evidence fit together – whether the totality makes sense. We'll test which theories "hold water."

Reasonable people can look at the same evidence and draw different conclusions. I'm not asking anything from you other than to join me with an open mind. Your conclusions may be different from mine. It's okay. We can still be friends. One thing is certain: you'll know a lot more about this unique figure, Jesus, after this journey. Let's go.

2

WHAT IS EVIDENCE?

We're going to get to the evidence about Jesus in short order because that's the focus of this book. There is a bit of groundwork we need to lay first. We'll fly through it. The first question is this: if we're going to be examining "evidence," what exactly is that?

Taunts are an important part of every person's childhood culture. In my wife's neighborhood, one of the prominent taunts was "I'm gonna cut you low." In mine, kids were always claiming they could defeat each other in various ways, from kicking a ball over a fence to wrestling an opponent into the ground. The standard counter-taunt, in my neighborhood, was this: "Oh yeah? Prove it." This called the question. It typically resulted in a fight, a kicked ball, or the original taunter backing down.

To modernize this example, "Prove It!" is now a very popular software application. It's used by employers to test job applicants. If an applicant says he can type 80 words a minute, he gets a chance to "Prove It!" If the applicant says she is proficient at Excel or Whiz Bang 3000, or speaking Farsi, "Prove It!" provides the confirmation. It's the modern equivalent of the playground counter-taunt.

Some things can be objectively proved. If the bully says he can make me "eat grass," and I improvidently say "oh yeah?

Prove it!" and he wrestles me to the ground and stuffs grass in my mouth, he has proved it. Typing 80 words a minute is an objective, real-time standard that can be proved on the spot.

Many other things in real life are very difficult to "prove." My father passed away a few years ago. In the last three years of his life, we suspected that he might have Alzheimer's disease. He went to a number of doctors, including several at the prestigious Mayo Clinic. They examined him, ran brain scans, and had him make drawings, write sentences, and perform executive functioning exercises. The result: inconclusive. We, as family members, made daily observations, gathering evidence. We had to make important decisions for his care and benefit in the midst of this inconclusiveness. It was hard, but important, and that's common in real life.

When we come to the evidence concerning Jesus, we're going to find that he lived 2,000 years ago in the Middle East. He pre-dated mass media, video, and the Internet. Events at the time were preserved orally and recorded in writing, but a lot of time has passed. Jerusalem, the city where many of the events of his life took place, was destroyed in 70 AD. Rome, where many official documents were likely stored, was almost completely destroyed by a fire in 64 AD. Some original evidence was inevitably lost.

To put this in perspective, US President John F. Kennedy was killed in 1963, one of the foremost events of my childhood. The event was filmed. A smoking gun was discovered. Yet substantial controversy about the event remains.

The point is, meeting the challenge to "prove it," when it comes to historical events, can be difficult. It is not impossible, though, as long as you understand what evidence and proof are.

FACT OR FICTION?

The term "proof" means different things to different people. To a mathematician, a "proof" is a procedure that conclusively establishes a mathematical proposition (such as a = b) with 100% certainty. To a scientist, "proof" involves experimentally testing a theory to determine that it accurately describes physical phenomena. In general, a scientific proof allows for some uncertainty. For example, Einstein's theory of general relativity has been shown to be true to 14 decimal places by scientific experiments. Many scientists will still say that the theory has not been "proved." This is an important part of the scientific method. You keep testing the hypothesis. Only with a very high level of evidence will it be "proved."

The law typically deals with events in the past. Somebody was murdered, or injured by a product – something happened, and the law seeks to determine what caused it and who is responsible. In criminal cases, the law demands a high level of proof of guilt: "beyond a reasonable doubt." Even this is not a 100% standard. There are always doubts. To acquit a criminal defendant, a "reasonable" doubt is required. In civil cases, the standard is lower. In general, to establish a claim or right, the proponent must prove the elements "by a preponderance of the evidence." Everyone is familiar with the "scales of justice." They illustrate the preponderance standard. Put all the evidence that tends to support a proposition on one side, the opposing evidence on the other, and if the scale tips even slightly, the weightier side wins. One might say the "weight of the evidence" supports one side or the other. Stated another way, a "preponderance of the evidence" means that a proposition is more likely true than untrue.

I will give you a small glimpse ahead. Though others have stated that the events concerning Jesus can be proved beyond any doubt, or beyond reasonable doubt, my lawyer-skeptic-engineer brain won't let me go there. Some things might meet that standard; for example, was Jesus a real person? That evidence is so strong that only someone with an ardent anti-faith could believe otherwise. When it comes to historical events like the death and resurrection of Jesus, I will only assume the "preponderance" standard. There is plenty of evidence, but I leave it to you to judge which way the scales tip.

What, then, is "evidence?" Literally every object on earth, every written and spoken word, is evidence of something. Even a thought could be evidence. The concept of evidence is extremely broad. It is so broad that the Federal Rules of Evidence, which govern my law practice to a great extent, don't bother to define it. The Federal Rules are more concerned with defining what is relevant and what is competent to be reviewed by a factfinder. In a jury trial, the Rules, as applied by a judge, act as a gatekeeper to prevent irrelevant or "bad" evidence from the jury's eyes.

Think of evidence as a potential component of proof. If proof is a wall, evidence is a brick, or a collection of bricks. Let's use the crucifixion of Jesus as an example. To build a wall of proof, we'll take bricks from several sources: eyewitness testimony, writings, archaeology, etc. We build the wall – the proof of Jesus's death on a cross – brick by brick. When it is done, we evaluate its strength. The strength is determined by the composition of individual bricks, the number of bricks, and how the bricks fit together. It is not necessary that each piece of evidence establish the whole case, just as a single brick is not a wall.

As I mentioned, courts have rules designed to filter out irrelevant and incompetent evidence. "Relevant" evidence is evidence that "has any tendency to make a fact more or less probable than it would be without the evidence" and "is of consequence in determining the action."[2] The competency rules provide thresholds to filter out unworthy evidence. For example, an expert cannot give opinion testimony unless he or she is qualified by education, training, and experience and follows analytical procedures that are typically followed in the expert's profession. Hearsay ("I know it because she told me") is generally not received, but there are several exceptions designed to ensure trustworthiness. A "statement against interest" ("she told me she killed him") is one of those exceptions. A person who says something against his own interest is unlikely to be lying.

One thing that is underappreciated about evidence is the strength or weakness of the counter-evidence. In most cases, there are two explanations for how or why an event occurred. There are two sides to every story. Because evidence is imperfect, you can almost always poke holes in the case for both sides. If there are some doubts about Explanation A, but the only alternative is Explanation B, which is full of holes, then Explanation A is likely to be true.

Let me illustrate that last point because it will be important to you in weighing the evidence. I had a case one time involving the tragic crash of a commercial jet on takeoff. The pilots had failed to extend the wing flaps and slats. The plane was equipped with a warning system that should have alerted the pilots that the wings weren't properly configured. The warning didn't sound. The evidence showed that electrical power was not flowing through the P40 circuit breaker associated with the warning system. There were no signs of an electrical overload that would cause the circuit breaker to "pop" open. That left two options: (1) the circuit breaker was defective, implicating the airframe manufacturer, or (2) the pilots had intentionally disabled the warning by "pulling" the circuit breaker.

The pilots had died in the crash, and the direct evidence of the pulling of the circuit breaker was scant. But there was substantial evidence about the other alternative – the integrity of the circuit breaker. Eminent experts testified on both sides, and I had the privilege of cross-examining the other side's expert, a professor from MIT. The P40 circuit breaker had been smashed to smithereens in the crash, but the pieces were found and they passed all the electrical tests. I got the MIT professor, who had tested the pieces, to admit that the P40, by standard tests, was "healthy."[3]

The jury found that the circuit breaker was not defective and that the pilots had committed willful misconduct. The strong evidence of a lack of defect meant that the pulling of the P40 breaker was the only plausible alternative. The weakness of one theory (defect) strengthened the other theory (pulling).

When it comes to the birth, life, death, and resurrection of Jesus, we will be looking at competing theories. We'll examine the following types of evidence:

1. What the Bible says – which may include or refer to eyewitness testimony

2. What other ancient writings say

3. What archaeology has unearthed

4. Physical evidence like tombs and the topography around Jerusalem

5. Social customs

Now that you've had a primer on evidence, you're ready for the next preliminary question.

3

THE BIBLE AND OTHER EVIDENCE

The Bible gives several descriptions of events in the life of Jesus. In general, there are four "gospels" written by Matthew, Mark, Luke, and John; there are several letters or "epistles" written by a converted Jewish scholar named Paul; and there are some additional letters by other writers, most notably Peter and John, two of Jesus's disciples. If the Bible is trustworthy, it is a rich source of evidence.

When you talk about the Bible, many people have gut-level reactions. Some revere it as a holy book, while others despise it without ever opening it. In between, there are many people who don't have a strong view about the Bible and don't know much about it. That's where I entered the fray 40 years ago – in the middle of the spectrum. I hadn't paid it much attention until I promised my friend I'd read it. I've now read every part of it multiple times. It won me over. I'm now on the "revere" side of the spectrum. But that was the result of truly getting to know it, and by examining the evidence about it. It wasn't my preconception.

Some people have said that "you can use the Bible to prove anything." I agree that people who have <u>abused</u> or misunderstood the Bible have used it to <u>try</u> to prove crazy things like slavery. Quoting Bible statements out of context, slavery proponents committed this sort of abuse. On the other hand, many of the people who led the abolition movements in the US and England, and ultimately prevailed, were strong Christians guided by Biblical principles. Both sides used the Bible to prove their points. One side was right and the other was wrong. One side used the Bible as proper evidence. The lesson is this: be careful how you use it, but don't cast it aside because others might abuse it.

My slavery example involved use of the Bible to prove right and wrong. The life of Jesus, however, is not such an issue. It's a historical issue – an issue of facts. Either the resurrection happened or it didn't. The testimony of eyewitnesses would be crucial bricks for our wall, and the Bible claims to record such testimony. It is, in the language of the Federal Rules of Evidence, "relevant." We therefore need to determine whether it's sufficiently trustworthy, i.e., whether the evidence it provides is reliable.

Thick books with lots of footnotes have been written about the reliability of the Bible. Every conceivable issue has been posed and answered. If you want to drill down on this, you should check out some of the books cited below. I'm going to cover only the basics, from my camera angle as a lawyer.

One of the things that jumps out at me as a Bible reader is how factual most parts of it are. Yes, there are miracles recounted, but even those are understated. The accounts of miracles are often reported in a "just the facts, ma'am" sort of way. Names of people and places are given. Corroborating facts are reported. Some of the authors appear to be like detectives filing investigation reports. Here is the opening to the book of Luke:

> "Many have undertaken to draw up an account of the things that have been fulfilled among us, just as they were handed down to us by those who

from the first were eyewitnesses and servants of the word. Therefore, since *I myself have carefully investigated everything from the beginning*, it seemed good also to me *to write an orderly account* for you, most excellent Theophilus, so that you may know the certainty of the things you have been taught." (Luke 1:1-4, italics added.)

Luke, it turns out, was a physician. Most of the doctors I know practice "evidence-based medicine," a term I find endearing. Doctors know how to investigate. They ask questions, they run lab tests, and they measure your blood pressure. They have an approach I find trustworthy.

Not surprisingly, Luke's writings have been scrutinized with the fine-tooth comb of archaeology, and he has passed with flying colors. Luke wrote both the gospel bearing his name and the book of Acts. In both, he goes into great detail about names, places, and obscure titles of officials. In the book of Acts, Luke explicitly names 32 countries, 54 cities, and nine islands. He gives the obscure titles of Jewish and Roman authorities such as priests, governors, and procurators. He relates his account to the wider context of world history. According to F. F. Bruce, a historian who does what Luke did "is courting trouble if he is not careful; he affords his critical readers so many opportunities for testing his accuracy."[4] Archaeology has repeatedly provided corroborating evidence of Luke's accuracy and has never contradicted him. Most of the ancient cities and other locations he mentions have been identified. Archaeology has resulted in Luke's accuracy as a historian being almost universally acknowledged.

Sir William Ramsay was a noted Scottish archaeologist who believed that the third gospel was written by someone other than Luke, sometime in the second century AD, and was not accurate historically. Setting out to prove these theories, Ramsay's archaeological discoveries instead convinced him of the truth of Luke's writings:

> "Luke is a historian of first rank; not merely are his statements of fact trustworthy; he is possessed of the true historic sense; he fixes his mind on the idea and plan that rules in the evolution of history; . . . In short, this author should be placed along with the very greatest of historians."
>
> "Luke's history is unsurpassed in respect of its trustworthiness. . . You may press the words of Luke in a degree beyond any other historian's, and they will stand the keenest scrutiny and the hardest treatment."[5]

Other eminent scholars have said similar things about Luke:

> "The general consensus of both liberal and conservative scholars is that Luke is very accurate as a historian. He's erudite, he's eloquent, his Greek approaches classical quality, he writes as an educated man and archaeological discoveries are showing over and over again that Luke is accurate in what he has to say."
>
> (John McRay, Ph.D., professor of New Testament and Archaeology at Wheaton College.)[6]
>
> "Now, all these evidences of accuracy are not accidental. A man whose accuracy can be demonstrated in matters where we are able to test it is likely to be accurate even where the means for testing him are not available. Accuracy is a habit

of mind, and we know from happy (or unhappy) experience that some people are habitually accurate just as others can be depended upon to be inaccurate. Luke's record entitles him to be regarded as a writer of habitual accuracy."

(F. F. Bruce, archaeologist and historian.)[7]

One of the things about Luke that rings true to me as a lawyer is that he had the <u>propensity</u> to be factual and truthful. This is one of the keys to witness examination. If a person is shown to be truthful on a dozen things that we can test, he's likely to have been truthful on the thirteenth thing, even if we can't test it. Conversely, if I catch a witness lying about five things, there's a good chance he was lying about other things. Propensity for truthfulness is important, and Luke has it.

Two of the other gospels were written by Matthew and John, disciples of Jesus. They were eyewitnesses. Peter, another disciple and eyewitness, wrote two New Testament letters. James, the half-brother of Jesus, wrote another one. One gospel was written by Mark, who was Peter's "interpreter," and wrote down everything Peter said about Jesus.[8]

In the 19th Century, it became popular to state that the gospels (Matthew, Mark, Luke, and John) were written after 150 AD, and therefore could not have been written by the disciples or their associates. This argument has essentially been laid to rest by dating evidence. The best example is the book of John. In the 1920s, a papyrus fragment was found in Egypt containing five verses from John chapter 18. Scholars have dated this fragment to the first quarter of the Second Century, i.e., 100-125 AD. John wrote his gospel in Ephesus, part of modern day Turkey, around 90 AD. By 125 AD or earlier, his gospel had been copied and distributed as far away as Egypt. This is another example of the stream of consistency between the Bible and archaeology.

It is now widely agreed that the New Testament books were written within the lifetimes of the eyewitnesses. But there is another check on the timing. The earliest writings about the life, death, and resurrection of Jesus were authored by Paul. Paul was martyred in the 60s AD; his writings covered the prior two decades and this has never been seriously doubted. One of his letters contains a fascinating passage:

> "For what I received I passed on to you as of first importance: that Christ died for our sins according to the Scriptures, that he was buried, that he was raised on the third day according to the Scriptures, and that he appeared to Cephas [Peter], and then to the Twelve. After that, he appeared to more than five hundred of the brothers at the same time, most of whom are still living, though some have fallen asleep. Then he appeared to James, then to all the apostles, and last of all he appeared to me also . . ." (1 Corinthians 15:3-8).

The verbs used by Paul in the beginning of this passage are technical rabbinical terms for receiving and transmitting holy traditions. The text has a parallelism and stylized content that is typical of an oral tradition. Paul uses the Aramaic name "Cephas" to refer to Peter, indicating an early origin. He uses other phrases that are not typical of Paul, such as "the Twelve," "the third day," and "he was raised." For these and other reasons, scholars are convinced that this is an early creed[9] that dates back to a time very shortly after the resurrection. It was preserved orally until Paul wrote it down. German historian Hans von Campenhausen says this creed "meets all the demands of historical reliability that could possibly be made of such a text."[10] Gary Habermas says it is an early creed that is "free from legendary contamination."[11]

FACT OR FICTION?

So who is this "Paul?" Originally named Saul, he was a highly educated man who studied under the famed rabbi Gamaliel. Paul's learning and reasoning abilities were renowned, and you can observe them yourself in his letters. Paul was definitely <u>not</u> a follower of Jesus during Jesus's lifetime. He zealously persecuted the Christian church, even supervising the stoning death of an early church leader. Paul was on his way to persecute Christians in Damascus when he saw a bright light and then heard the voice of Jesus. Straight away, he began investigating the historical basis for the death and resurrection of Jesus.

Paul did what I would have done. According to Paul's letter to the Galatians, he spent 15 days with Peter, "*interviewing*" him. The Greek word in the original writing, *historeo*, indicates an investigation, with Paul in the role of examiner, asking questions and getting answers. He also met with James, the half-brother of Jesus. Thus Paul, like Luke, was an investigator, piecing together the facts from eyewitnesses. At first the most ardent of skeptics, Paul spread the news of Christianity far and wide on the backbone of investigated facts. His letters and the second half of the book of Acts testify to this.

As a trial lawyer, I like to have my witnesses and the jury, to the extent possible, interact with the evidence. I like to have them touch physical evidence and give demonstrations about how things work. I want them to read the documents, not just look at snippets. Why do I do this? Because you are more likely to be convinced if you see for yourself rather than just taking my word for it. Thus, I invite you readers to put this book down and go read the gospel of Luke and Paul's epistle to the Romans for yourselves. See if I'm right. Are these good writers? Are they logical thinkers? Do they seem reasonable? Are they trustworthy?

I take great comfort in the fact that the Bible itself validates the "see for yourself" approach. Not one of the disciples initially believed that Jesus would be raised from the dead. They weren't expecting it. They were cowering in fear. One disciple, Thomas, refused to believe the verbal reports that Jesus was alive. He said "unless I see the nail marks in his hands and put my finger where the nails were, and put my hand into his side, I will not believe" (John 20:24). That would have been me. I need evidence. Jesus, instead of scolding Thomas, said, "Put your finger here." Thomas touched the wounds in Jesus's hands and side, and immediately believed. That would have been me, too. Some skeptics will hold out in spite of incontrovertible evidence. Most, like me, will come around when the scales tip.

There is a lot more to be said about the reliability of the Bible, but I want to stay focused. This is a study of the evidence concerning Jesus, not concerning the Bible itself. The Bible is evidence. It is not the only type of evidence we'll be looking at. In fact, one of the important exercises we're going to undertake is to see if the Biblical evidence is corroborated (confirmed) by extra-Biblical evidence. Here is what I recommend as we proceed. Consider the Bible to be evidence of what Jesus did and experienced. Examine what it has to say. Don't consider it conclusive by itself. See if it holds up when the other evidence comes in.

4

Voir Dire: God and Miracles

Before people are selected to be on a jury, they go through a screening process to determine if they have biases that will prevent them from fairly examining the evidence. The lawyers get to ask questions to determine the extent of any biases. This process is called "voir dire," and most seasoned trial lawyers will tell you that trials are often won or lost in jury selection.

The term "voir dire" combines the French words for "true" and "to say." You are probably pronouncing it incorrectly unless you are French. Most American lawyers say "vwahr – deer." In the South, they say "vorr – dyer." Voir dire is important because many people have firmly held presuppositions that can hinder the search for truth. We use the term "prejudice," which means to pre-judge. You're not supposed to do that. A juror who pre-judges the case won't listen fairly to the evidence.

We all have biases. Most jurors can set them aside, but if they can't, then they should not serve. For example, if you believe that all criminal defendants are guilty because the police would not arrest an innocent person, you should not serve on a criminal jury. If you believe that the police are oppressors who routinely arrest innocent people, then you shouldn't serve. Most people, by the way, are between these two extremes in their thinking.

Let me ask you two questions to help determine your baseline approach:

- Do you believe in God?

- Do you believe in miracles?

If your answer is no, or you're not sure, but you're willing to look at the evidence, then you're on my jury. I'll show you the evidence and you can decide for yourself. However, if you are unwaveringly committed to the non-existence of God, and are 100% opposed to the notion that anything supernatural has ever occurred, then you won't be able to fairly weigh the evidence. These two questions are my "voir dire." They're a litmus test for presupposition.

This is a book about Jesus, so you may legitimately ask: what do these two questions have to do with Jesus? Well, the Bible recounts several things about Jesus that people would call "supernatural" or "miraculous." Is it possible that he rose from the dead? That's a supernatural event. There's substantial evidence on that point, but it won't be of interest to you if you've ruled out the possibility of resurrection (or miracles in general) in advance.

All right, by now you've answered the voir dire questions. I'm going to assume you believe in the <u>possibility</u> that God exists and that miracles can happen, but you're withholding judgment until you see the evidence. Good! That's what jurors are supposed to do.

A person who believes only in material things is called, logically, a "materialist." The percentage of materialists in the general population is actually quite small. I don't want to demean them; most of them are very intelligent. But they will not consider any evidence that leads to the conclusion that a miracle has happened. They don't believe in miracles, or the supernatural, or God. They have made up their minds in advance, as a philosophical tenet. You and I can definitely be friends if this is what you believe. But as your friend, I will advise you to put this book down. You'd be wasting your time to hear me present the evidence.

Most people are, like me, skeptical of any event that is claimed to be miraculous but are willing to look at the evidence. We're willing to conclude that sometimes, rarely, miracles may have occurred. Polls show that over 90% of Americans believe in God and 80% believe in miracles.[12] Pollster George Gallup claimed that he could prove God's existence "statistically." Personally, I'm not buying that kind of proof. The existence of God is not determined by a majority vote. Even if <u>no one</u> believed in God, He could still exist. He either exists or He doesn't, and our belief or lack of it doesn't determine reality.

The skeptic might say, "Most Americans are stupid, or deceived." Alas, there may be some truth to this. But don't discount the views of common people. G.K. Chesterton, a man described as a "colossal genius,"[13] came away from serving on a jury with the following observation:

> "Our civilization has decided, and very justly decided, that determining the guilt or innocence of men is a thing too important to be trusted to trained men. If it wishes for light upon that awful matter, it asks men who know no more law than I know, but who can feel the things that I felt in the jury box. When it wants a library catalogued, or the solar system discovered, or any trifle of that kind, it uses up its specialists. But when it wishes anything done which is really serious, it collects twelve of the ordinary men standing round. The

same thing was done, if I remember right, by the Founder of Christianity."[14]

Amen, that's the world I live in. The views of ordinary people count for something. And the numbers are so lopsided, the honest investigator is compelled to ask <u>why</u> all these people believe in God and miracles. Is there a rational basis for their belief?

New books are written every week on this subject. I'm going to cover it only in summary fashion. If you want to drill down, I recommend *Can Man Live Without God?* by Ravi Zacharias. The book is a witty, eminently readable defense of belief in God. Zacharias is a brilliant man, born and raised in India, an atheist until the age of 17 when he became a Christian after reading the book of John. *Can Man Live Without God?* summarizes other belief systems and compares them to Christianity.

Here are the evidences for the existence of God and non-material reality that I find most intriguing:

1. **<u>Existence of Life and other Things.</u>** You exist. I exist. Something, instead of nothing, exists. How can anything exist if there is no God? Science confirms this logic. Science tells us the universe had a beginning and that it began with a "big bang."[15] But what caused the bang? Some chemicals came together. Where did the chemicals come from? If there is an answer to that, there is another question, then another, then another: where did that come from? Logically, the first cause must have come from something outside nature, something un-, pre-, or super-natural.

Similarly, the origin of life is an intractable problem for those who deny the supernatural. Louis Pasteur conducted one of the most famous scientific experiments of all time. If you don't know Pasteur, you should read about his life. He was an incredibly accomplished scientist whose work has saved the lives of millions of people.[16] Pasteur set out to test the theory of "spontaneous generation" – the notion that living organisms could arise from non-living things. Using boiled liquid in a curved-neck flask, Pasteur proved once and for all that **living things come from other living things, and the generation of living things from non-living things is impossible:**

> No, there is now no circumstance known in which it can be affirmed that microscopic beings came into the world without germs, without parents similar to themselves. Those who affirm it have been duped by illusions, by ill-conducted experiments, spoilt by errors that they either did not perceive or did not know how to avoid.[17]

The concept of spontaneous generation has never recovered from Pasteur's mortal blow.

Ponder this for a minute: living things come only from other living things. Where, then, did the first living thing come from? It must have come into existence through a cause acting outside of nature – a "super"natural cause. This is as close to QED proof as you can get in the world of science. Remember how I said that the strength of a case is increased when the opposing evidence is weak? That's the case here. Scientists committed to materialism have been trying for decades to find a way for life to have arisen spontaneously. They've only met dead ends. Some Nobel Prize-winning scientists have fallen back on a theory called "directed panspermia" as a way around the "origin of life" problem.[18] This theory proposes that "seeds" of life were planted on earth by aliens from another planet! Where did the seeds and the aliens come from? "Nothing illustrates more clearly just how intractable a problem the origin of life has become than the fact that world authorities can seriously toy with the idea of panspermia."[19] With directed panspermia, we are in the realm of science fiction, not reality.

I think we can give God the credit for the origin of life. You know who else concluded that? Louis Pasteur.

2. **The "Fingerprints" of God.** Few people have seen God. You and I are not among them. Astronauts have been to outer space, and telescopes have been sent far out into the universe. Some people have reported, "I did not see God there." Others have said they <u>did</u> see God there. I'm skeptical of that. Despite the fact that Michelangelo painted a picture of God on the ceiling of the Sistine Chapel, most people would agree that God is invisible. That is one of His attributes. He can take on visible forms if He wants to, because He is God, but usually He's invisible.

Aha, says the skeptic. This very attribute belies God's existence. The materialist believes only in things that can be seen, touched and measured. God is not material; therefore, He does not exist. The problem with this argument is that it is circular. If you start with the assumption that only material things exist, then you have assumed away the existence of God, you haven't proved His non-existence. An assumption is not proof. The question is whether the initial assumption is correct.

I enjoy a comic strip called "Pooch Café" by Paul Gilligan. A male Bichon Frise dog named "Poo-Poo" has a continuing hard time with a female Bull Mastiff named "Droolia." Droolia is so named because she drools prolifically. Droolia likes to kiss Poo-Poo, who hates being covered in slobber. One day Poo-Poo is in his yard and announces to Droolia, who is on the sidewalk, that his master has installed an "invisible fence" – "good luck trying to kiss me now." Droolia proceeds to cross the invisible fence line and cover Poo-Poo in slobber. Poo-Poo looks defeated and says, "I knew I was stupid to believe in an 'invisible fence.'" In the final panel, Poo-Poo crosses the fence line and gets zapped. (If you don't know about invisible dog fences, they don't work unless the dog is wearing a special collar; Poo-Poo was wearing one, while Droolia wasn't.) The moral of the story: don't disbelieve in God just because He is invisible.

We cannot "see" the wind, but we can see trees bending over in a hurricane. I once worked on a lawsuit involving a birth defect in the brain known as a "cavernous angioma" that can seep blood, resulting in a stroke. You can't see the angioma itself on any type of brain scan – the blood vessels that comprise it are microscopic and the blood inside moves too slowly. However, the neuroradiologist can see the signature of a cavernous angioma on magnetic resonance imaging (MRI). It has a well-recognized pattern of bright and dark spots often described as a "popcorn" effect representing blood products of varying stages of breakdown. When the neuroradiologist sees the popcorn, he knows there is probably a cavernous angioma there, even though the angioma itself is invisible. This is really the essence of investigative work. Police dust for fingerprints at the crime scene and they find evidence left by a murderer who is nowhere in sight.

Even if God is not ordinarily visible, has He left fingerprints? Do we see His signature? We live in a privileged generation. Scientific discoveries about the universe have taken a huge leap forward. In 1965, Arno Penzias and Robert Wilson discovered that there is a "background radiation" in the universe and it is not uniform – it has "ripples." The implication: the universe had a beginning; it wasn't just "always there." Almost every scientist now agrees.

Penzias, who won the Nobel Prize with Wilson, understands the logical and theological implications of the scientific evidence he discovered: *"The best data we have concerning the Big Bang are exactly what I would have predicted had I nothing to go on but the five books of Moses, the Psalms, the Bible as a whole."*[20] Astrophysicist Hugh Ross calls the background radiation ripples *"the Fingerprint of God."*[21]

There are many other scientific examples of God's "fingerprints." One of my favorites is the "anthropic principle." The universe is "fine tuned" to support life – a slight adjustment in any one of 70 physical parameters (such as the size of the sun, the distance of earth from the sun, the axial tilt of the earth and the strength of the forces of gravity and electromagnetism) would make life impossible. Who did the tuning? The scientific problems faced by those trying to disprove God are staggering.

The mapping of the human "genome" – full set of human DNA – was completed in 2001. Human DNA consists of 3.16 billion nucleotide bases that appear to be exquisitely, rather than randomly, arranged. Words used by scientists to describe DNA include "code," "recipe," or "instructions" on how to make human proteins. DNA is like the software for making human hardware. The obvious question is, who wrote the code? Who made the recipe? Francis Collins, Director of the Human Genome Institute, says, "You can't survey that, going through page after page without a sense of awe. I can't help but look at those pages and have a vague sense that this is giving me a glimpse of God's mind."[22]

Wait a minute; this is a lot of science. Have you heard it said that science disproves God? Some people – materialists – have tried to argue that. I'm a math-science geek who strongly believes in scientific evidence. So are the scientists I've been quoting. I am not going to overstate the case by saying that science "proves" God. I'll just say that there is plenty of scientific evidence to make it rational to believe in God. Science does not disprove God; it points to Him.

3. **Order and Chaos; Good and Evil; Truth and Beauty.** What is your view as to whether there is "order" in the universe? The materialist who believes that we are the result of purely random, accidental, chaotic processes would have no trouble explaining disorder, chaos, and randomness in the universe. There is definitely some of that. But there is also a great deal of order – planets move in predictable orbits, Halley's comet and locusts appear right on schedule, apples grow on apple trees, and snakes give birth to baby snakes. Vera Kistiakowsky, MIT physicist, has said, "The exquisite order displayed by our scientific understanding of the physical world calls for the divine."[23] Galileo said that the universe "is written in the language of mathematics." Molecular biologist Michael Denton says that "it is primarily because the laws of nature can be described in simple mathematical forms that nature is inherently decipherable."[24] In other words, the universe speaks a language that man understands. Yale philosophy professor Jonathan Lear summarized this nicely:

> "The inquiry into nature revealed the world as meant to be known; the inquiry into man's soul revealed him as a being who is meant to be a knower. Man and the world are, as it were, meant for each other."[25]

Where did all this order come from, if there is no God?

Do you believe that truth exists? Morality? Evil and good? If you believe any of that, then you believe in things that transcend the material world.

Some people have said that the existence of evil disproves God – a loving God would not allow evil. There are good answers to this allegation, although I acknowledge that it is a tough nut to crack. Step back from the details for a minute and consider the question itself. It presumes the existence of "evil." I submit that to acknowledge the existence of evil is to acknowledge the supernatural. With atheism, there is "no evil and no good."[26] If you believe there is good in this world – or evil, or both – then atheism cannot be true.

In my job as a lawyer, I have seen plenty of evil and good. I have dedicated my *pro bono* efforts to assisting victims of human trafficking. Human trafficking is modern slavery. It involves forcing another human to work through violence or coercion and, agonizingly, a large portion of it involves children and the sex trade. A greater evil is hard to imagine, and it is more prevalent now than at any time in history. But for us to call human trafficking "evil" – as every rational person would do – implies the existence of morality, a standard against which conduct is measured. No such standard exists for the materialist.

Dr. Martin Luther King, Jr., in his Nobel Peace Prize acceptance speech, said, "I refuse to accept the notion that man is mere flotsam and jetsam in the river of life . . . unable to respond to the eternal oughtness that forever confronts him."[27] I like the phrase "eternal oughtness." Man is eternally, constantly, confronted with "oughts" – things he knows are right. These are the words of a theist.

If you have seen evil, as I have, then you are not a materialist. My anti-trafficking work has also shown me the existence of "good" in the world. I work alongside people who put their lives and careers in danger to help victims and fight modern slavery. There's no material profit in their work. They do it "altruistically," with no thought of benefitting themselves.

Materialism cannot explain altruism. And if there is "good" in the world, where did it come from?

Most people believe that there is <u>both</u> evil and good in the world, both order and disorder. The existence of God, as described in the Bible, accounts for both. God is the author of the "good" and the "order." But the universe and man are in a "broken" state through no fault of God's. In fact, God has initiated a solution. Jesus is the solution, but I'm getting ahead of myself again.

Do you have a conscience? If you do, you can't be a materialist. The French philosopher Voltaire used to throw dinner parties for his atheist friends. He implored them, however, not to talk about atheist philosophies around the servants because he was afraid if they stopped believing in God, they would murder him in his sleep or steal all his possessions.

Do you believe in beauty? Is there something in a work of art that transcends the dabs of paint on canvas? Is there something in music that speaks to your soul? The great conductor Leonard Bernstein said this:

> Beethoven broke all the rules, and turned out pieces of breathtaking rightness. Rightness – that's the word! When you get the feeling that whatever note succeeds the last is the only possible note that can rightly happen at that instant, in that context, then chances are you're listening to Beethoven. * * * Our boy has the real goods, the stuff from Heaven, the power to make you feel at the finish: *Something is right in the world.*[28]

If there is a "rightness" in music, a beauty in art, then my view is that it is not all due to random chance. Beethoven, by the way, considered his art to be a sacred trust placed upon him by his Creator.[29]

The point of all of this is that there seems to be a reality that transcends the material world. There seems to be more than randomness and chance.

4. **The Meaning of Life.** Do you wonder about the meaning of life? Why are you here, what are you supposed to do? Many people ask these questions. In fact, if you don't ask them, I have to wonder if there is something wrong with you.

In the Bible, the book of Ecclesiastes was written by one of the wisest men to walk the earth – King Solomon. He looked for meaning in wealth, fame, and pleasure, and like many who walked the earth after him, he found it all to be "vanity." It's not enough. It doesn't satisfy. We thirst for something more than what the material world can give us.

Why does man search for meaning, if there is no meaning and never was any? Why does man seek life after death? Where did man get the idea of God? If there is no meaning in life, as the atheists say, then why do we yearn for meaning? Why do we despair when confronted with the notion of meaninglessness? Why are we dissatisfied with meaninglessness as an answer, and enriched by meaning? It could be that life is not meaningless. God provides a meaning and the desire for meaning. If you have such a desire, atheism is not for you.

In his book *Rumors of Another World: What on Earth Are We Missing?*, Philip Yancey writes that we search for more because there is more. There is another world, intertwined with the material world, and there are evidences of it everywhere. We live among clues, "like rescuers who sift through pieces of stained glass shattered by a bomb."[30] Some people turn off their antennae and miss out. The "other world" makes the material world a richer place.

It sounds presumptuous to say that something doesn't exist if I can't see, hear, or touch it. Why stop investigating at the end of that box? Maybe there's more. Look through the stained glass shards and decide for yourself. But turning your back on the clues seems an unwise and unhappy choice. I don't know about you, but if there's more, I really want to find it. I want to experience it.

Let's leave this section with a reiteration. There is no absolute proof for or against miracles or God's existence. There are opposing views on every point. The vast majority of people have found that there is at least a reasonable basis for belief. So, if you're not convinced yet, it's perfectly fine. Just keep an open mind. Check your presuppositions.

Now we can move on to the real stuff – the evidence about Jesus.

5

IS JESUS REAL?

Let's start with an easy question. Did Jesus really live, or is he a legend – the figment of a creative imagination? The existence of Jesus is a historical question that can be answered with hard facts. There is so much evidence, in fact, that only extreme skeptics dispute the existence of Jesus.

Biblical Evidence

Virtually the entire New Testament teaches that Jesus was a real person who walked the earth. He lived in what is now Israel. He was born in Bethlehem, near Jerusalem (Matthew 2:1; Luke 2:4-7). The Bible tells us he was born during the reign of Herod the Great in Palestine (Matthew 2:1). He lived during the reigns of the Roman emperors Augustus (31 BC - 14 AD) and Tiberius (14-37 AD), both of whom are mentioned in the New Testament (Luke 2:1 and 3:1). Names of contemporary people, places and events abound.

Eight or nine authors wrote the New Testament.[31] Some of them wrote from personal experience and observation. At least three of the writers were disciples of Jesus who followed him around for three years. All of the writers suffered persecution and/or death for their belief in Jesus. Much of that persecution is recorded in the Bible itself. It isn't plausible that they went to all that trouble for something they knew to be a fiction.

Extra-Biblical Evidence

There are several direct references to Jesus in non-Christian writings, including those of Romans and Jews. First Century Roman historian Tacitus refers to Jesus and his execution by Pontius Pilate during the reign of the Roman emperor Tiberius. Tacitus was the most prominent Roman historian of the period, and he is considered one of the greatest historians of all time. He lived from 56-117 AD. He was extremely thorough in his research, and drew upon the works of earlier historians, whose works are not available to us today. He relied on material from the public records, official reports, and contemporary comments. He also turned, as far as he felt necessary, to the Roman Senate's records, the official journal, and such firsthand information as speeches, personal memoirs and military memoirs. In his *Annals of Imperial Rome*, Tacitus wrote about the fire that destroyed most of Rome in 64 AD:

> "Yet no human effort, no princely largess nor offerings to the gods could make that infamous rumor disappear that [Roman Emperor] Nero had somehow ordered the fire. Therefore, to abolish the rumor, Nero substituted as culprits, and punished with the utmost refinements of cruelty, a class of men, loathed for their vices, whom the crowd styled **Christians. Christus, from whom they got their name, had been executed by sentence of the procurator Pontius Pilate when Tiberius was emperor**; and the pernicious superstition was checked for a short time, only to break out afresh, not only in Judea, the home of the plague, but in Rome itself, where all the horrible and shameful things in the world collect and find a home. Therefore, first those were seized who admitted their faith, and then, using the information they

provided, a vast multitude were convicted, not so much for the crime of burning the city, but for hatred of the human race. And perishing they were additionally made into sports: they were killed by dogs by having the hides of beasts attached to them, or they were nailed to crosses or set aflame, and, when the daylight passed away, they were used as nighttime lamps. Nero gave his own gardens for this spectacle and performed a Circus game, in the habit of a charioteer mixing with the plebs or driving about the race-course. Even though they were clearly guilty and merited being made the most recent example of the consequences of the crime, people began to pity these sufferers, because they were consumed not for the public good but on account of the fierceness of one man." (Emphasis added.)[32]

Clearly, Tacitus was no friend of Christianity – he was a critic and an opponent. Yet his account provides rich details about Jesus and his followers. Tacitus corroborates many important points from the New Testament: (a) Jesus was a real person; (b) Jesus was executed by Pilate in the reign of the emperor Tiberius; (c) shortly after Jesus's death, the movement named for him "broke out" in Judea and spread quickly to Rome, where it had a significant presence by 64 AD; and (d) Christians were persecuted with ferocity by the Romans because of their faith.

Other Roman writings mention Christ and Christians, and we will explore them in later chapters.

Jewish writings also attest to the life and death of Jesus. Perhaps the most famous comes from Flavius Josephus, a First Century Jewish historian. Josephus wrote one passage about the execution of James, "the brother of Jesus, who was called the Christ."³³ He also wrote a passage directly about Jesus:

> "About this time there lived Jesus, a wise man *if indeed one ought to call him a man*. For he was one who wrought surprising feats and was a teacher of such people as accept the truth gladly. He won over many Jews and many of the Greeks. *He was the Messiah*. When Pilate, upon hearing him accused by men of the highest standing among us, had condemned him to be crucified, those who had in the first place come to love him did not cease. *On the third day he appeared to them restored to life. For the prophets of God had prophesied these and myriads of other marvellous things about him*. And the tribe of the Christians, so called after him, has still up to now, not disappeared."³⁴

Some people assert that the italicized phrases were added by a later editor, while others insist they are genuine. Even if we ignore those phrases, the writing of Josephus confirms the existence of Jesus and many basic facts about him.

There are other early Jewish writings referring to Jesus. There are also letters of skeptics and followers. Every early source accepts Jesus as a real person; none of them asserts that he is fictional.

Encyclopedia Britannica contains an extensive article on Jesus. It reviews the various historical sources and says, "These independent accounts prove that in ancient times even the opponents of Christianity never doubted the historicity of Jesus, which was disputed for the first time and on inadequate grounds by several authors at the end of the 18th, during the 19th, and at the beginning of the 20th centuries."³⁵

There are still a few people today who say that Jesus is a myth, but their position is contradicted by the facts and must be viewed as unreasonable.

6

THE BIRTH OF JESUS

Larry King, the noted television interviewer of the famous, was asked what question he would pose to Jesus if he could interview him. King replied, "I would like to ask Him if He was indeed virgin born, because the answer to that question would explain history for me."[36]

If Jesus was truly virgin born, that means he was more than just a man. It would mean that miracles happen. If that fact is true, it would "explain history."

Biblical Evidence

The Bible says that Jesus was born to Jewish parents. His mother, Mary, was "a virgin pledged to be married to a man named Joseph," at the time she was told by an angel that she would give birth to the Son of God (Luke 1:27). Before Mary and Joseph "came together," she was "found to be with child through the Holy Spirit" (Matthew 1:18). Joseph knew he wasn't the father and "had in mind to divorce her quietly" (Matthew 1:19). An angel then appeared to Joseph and told him that "What is conceived in her is from the Holy Spirit" (Matthew 1:20). Joseph took Mary as his wife, but "had no union with her until she gave birth to a son" (Matthew 1:24-25).

There is an additional side to the virgin birth accounts – in the Old Testament. Isaiah 7:14, written more than 700 years before the birth of Jesus, says of the coming Messiah (Savior), "Therefore the Lord himself will give you a sign; The virgin shall be with child and will give birth to a son, and will call him Immanuel." Clearly, the Messiah would not be an angelic being; nor would he arrive on earth fully grown – he would be born into the human race as a baby.

There is a serious debate about the word "virgin" in the Isaiah passage. The Hebrew word used by Isaiah is *almah*, which means young woman, maiden, or virgin. It is used in Genesis 24:43 to refer to an unmarried maiden. It does not <u>necessarily</u> signify technical virginity in the sense of never having had sexual relations. There is another word, *bethulah*, which could have been used to unequivocally signify technical virginity. Nevertheless, *almah* is a term that normally implies virginity (in that society, unmarried maidens were usually virgins), and New Testament writers Luke and Matthew, schooled in Hebrew, understood it in that sense.

Personally, I don't get worked up over this debate. Either way, the Isaiah passage predicts a birth just like that of Jesus. The New Testament states very clearly that Jesus was born of a young woman, Mary, and that Mary was both unmarried and a physiological virgin at the time she conceived Jesus (Luke 1:26-35; Matthew 1:18-25).

Extra-Biblical Evidence

That Jesus was "born" doesn't give pause to many people. Here's some evidence you can observe today: people still commemorate that birth. When I turned on my computer to write this chapter, it gave me the date: 2016. Two thousand and sixteen years – since what? Since the birth of Jesus. Our calendars, even today, are based on his birth.

Another piece of evidence that you can see and touch today is in the modern town of Bethlehem. You can go, as I have, to the Church of the Nativity and see the grotto where it is claimed that Jesus was born. I have seen it. It seems consistent with the Biblical account, and some historical investigation tends to back it up as the likely location. I wouldn't call it strong evidence, because there are gaps in the historical record, but it's tangible.

The Quran, the holy book of Islam, states that Jesus was born of a virgin.[37] This means that the religions of 60% of the world's population (Christianity and Islam) ascribe to the virgin birth.

An interesting recurring theme of the ancient Jewish Talmud is that Jesus was a "bastard" son of a married woman. He is sometimes referred to in the Talmudic writings as "Yeshu ben Padera" or "ben Pantera." Pantera may be the name of a Roman soldier who is supposed to have been Jesus's true father. Alternatively, "Pantera" may be a play on the Greek word for virgin (*parthenos*). Joseph Klausner, a Jewish historian, says, "The illegitimate birth of Jesus was a current idea among the Jews."[38] Illegitimacy would be a human or skeptical interpretation of the virgin birth. It recognizes that Mary got pregnant before getting married, and Joseph was not the father.

The writings of the Greek philosopher Celsus show some of the arguments that early skeptics were using against Jesus. Celsus lived in the Second Century and his writings do not survive, except as quoted by the Third Century Christian writer Origen. Celsus wrote that Jesus was a bastard whose mother was "a poor Jewess who. . .had been turned out of doors by her husband, who was a carpenter by trade, on being convicted of adultery."[39]

Analysis

As an evidence evaluator, I find it significant that from early times, the skeptical "spin" was that Jesus was illegitimate. If Jesus was truly conceived with no human father in the womb of a virgin, how would that look to the outside world? The natural presumption would be that Mary had engaged in immorality. This point is driven home in the 2006 movie *The Nativity Story*. Mary turns up pregnant as a teenager in the small Jewish village of Nazareth. She is the only one who knows that she has never slept with a man. She is the only one who knows that the baby in her womb is the child of God. To everyone else, her pregnancy is awful news. Her friends are scared for her. Her father is outraged. The people in the village want to stone her. These are natural reactions to the evidence. I find the illegitimacy stories to be just what I'd expect in the circumstances.

Why didn't the villagers stone Mary to death? That was the unavoidable penalty for Mary's apparent crime. Her enlarged belly would ordinarily be conclusive proof. In *The Nativity Story*, Joseph comes to Mary's defense. It seems realistic to me that there was a pause in the action. Mary insisted on her innocence and the people of the village knew her to be a good, moral girl. Joseph gave his evidence – I didn't sleep with her, and I believe her that she didn't sleep with anyone else. Her parents and friends provided character evidence. It's plausible that the villagers didn't stone Mary because the evidence convinced a number of people that maybe she hadn't committed immorality after all.

In the end, we have significant corroboration for the Biblical statements that Jesus was born in unusual circumstances, and that Joseph was not the real father. It would be difficult to go further than this with hard evidence. Had modern doctors been present, they could have confirmed whether Mary was a technical virgin. Modern DNA evidence might have determined paternity. We're used to that kind of proof from watching *CSI* on television. But it wasn't available then to confirm or deny the Biblical account of virginity. All other aspects of the Biblical accounts hold up. Remember, when a writer has a <u>propensity</u> for truthfulness, and has been corroborated multiple times, we tend to trust him on points where there is no other evidence available to us.

Is the concept of a virgin birth logical? This is why I asked first whether you believe in miracles. A virgin birth is a miracle – it's supernatural. If you strictly adhere to the notion that no supernatural thing has ever happened, then no, the virgin birth is not logical to you. With God, however, "all things are possible" (Matt. 19:26). There is no necessary logical disconnect between the existence of God and a virgin birth.

<u>Why</u> was Jesus born of a virgin? This requires some reasoned speculation. Perhaps God wanted the coming of the Messiah to be associated with a spectacular miracle to gain people's attention. Perhaps it was to fulfill the prophecy of Isaiah, which is another spectacular thing. My take on the virgin birth is this: God knew that there would be controversy and danger associated with this birth. That's the world He chose to enter, and it's <u>why</u> He chose to enter it. The world was broken. God could have arrived on earth as a grown adult, avoiding all the dirt and danger of pregnancy, birth, and childhood. But He came to save <u>people</u> who all experience that stuff. He could have come into a palace and lived like a king; but instead, He was born in a stable, put into an animal's feeding trough, and grew up learning to be a carpenter.

Philip Yancey said it better than I can. "Nine months of awkward explanations, the lingering scent of scandal – it seems that God arranged the most humiliating circumstances possible for his entrance, as if to avoid any charge of favoritism." God, he said, "played by the rules, harsh rules."[40]

There may be theological reasons why God chose an extraordinary conception for His son, but I'm persuaded by the practical reasons. It makes sense to me. Not only does it make sense, its implications are monumental. In the words of Larry King, it "explain[s] history."

7

THE LIFE OF JESUS

The common view of Jesus – the view I held before I investigated at the age of 19 – is that he was a good man and an exemplary moral teacher. Let's look at the evidence of Jesus's life to see if these points bear out. Let's look at what he taught.

Biblical Evidence

Jewish Ancestry: Matthew chapter 1 gives the genealogy of Jesus through his mother Mary, which traces back to King David, and all the way back to Jacob, Isaac, and Abraham. Luke chapter 3 gives a separate genealogy through Joseph, showing that Joseph also was related to David and Abraham. Jesus's parents were Jewish and raised him under Jewish law and tradition, having him circumcised and consecrated to the Lord (Luke 2:21-23) and observing Jewish feasts and festivals (Luke 2:41). In physical appearance, Jesus looked like a Jewish man (John 4:9).

From Nazareth: Within a few years after Jesus was born in Bethlehem, his family moved to Nazareth, where they had probably lived previously (Matthew 2:23; Luke 2:39). He grew up in Nazareth (Luke 3:51). Nazareth was in the region of Galilee in northern Israel (Matthew 2:22-23).

Forerunner – John the Baptist: John, known as "the Baptist," was the son of Elizabeth and Zechariah (Luke 1:5-25). Elizabeth and Mary were cousins, and so Jesus and John the Baptist were related to each other (Luke 1:36). As an adult, John lived in the desert. In the 15th year of Tiberius (29 AD), John went into the regions around the Jordan River preaching "a baptism of repentance" (Luke 3:3). John was asked whether he was the Christ (Messiah), and he said that he was not, but that the Christ was coming (Luke 3:15-16). John's baptizing ministry, which was designed to prepare the people to receive the coming Messiah, is detailed in all four gospels (Matthew 3; Mark 1; Luke 3; John 1). All four gospels record that John baptized Jesus. John was imprisoned because he rebuked Herod Antipas, tetrarch of Galilee, for marrying his niece/sister-in-law (Luke 3:19). Eventually, Herod Antipas ordered John the Baptist to be executed (Luke 9:7-9).

A Great Teacher: The teachings of Jesus pervade the gospels and are repeated through the entire New Testament. One of the more famous groupings of his sayings is in what is referred to as the "Sermon on the Mount" in Matthew 5-7. Jesus also taught in the synagogues of Galilee (Matthew 4:23). People called him "rabbi" and "teacher" (e.g., John 3:2). He was known as a man of "wisdom" (e.g., Luke 2:52). Even his enemies acknowledged that he was "a man of integrity. . . who teach[es] the way of God in accordance with the truth" (Matthew 22:16). An examination of his teachings shows the highest moral code known to man.

Disciples: Jesus specifically called 12 disciples to follow him (Matthew 4; Mark 3; Luke 5; John 1). There were others who also followed, and were called "disciples" (Luke 6:13; John 6:66). The original 12 are sometimes referred to as "apostles" or "the Twelve" to distinguish them from other disciples (Mark 3:14; Luke 6:13).

Miracles: The gospels record approximately three dozen miracles by Jesus, falling roughly into three categories: (1) healing the sick and lame; (2) raising two persons from the dead; and (3) overruling natural processes in other ways, such as calming a storm, turning water into wine, and walking on water.

Called Christ, The Messiah: Jesus claimed to be the Messiah, the Christ, the Son of God, equal to God. Other people also called him these things. I'm going to spend some time on this because I think it is both astonishing and critical. The <u>identity</u> of Jesus is one of the most misunderstood things about Christianity. It is also one of the most important things.

Fyodor Dostoyevsky, the Russian writer, said, "The most pressing question on the problem of faith is whether a man as a civilized being. . .can believe in the divinity of the Son of God, Jesus Christ, for therein rests the whole of our faith."[41]

The gospel of Luke records that in one of his first public appearances, Jesus went to the synagogue in his hometown. He was asked to teach from the (Old Testament) scriptures, and the scroll of the prophet Isaiah was handed to him. He unrolled it and read as follows (Isaiah 61:1-2):

> 'The Spirit of the Lord is on me, because he has anointed me to preach good news to the poor. He has sent me to proclaim freedom for the prisoners and recovery of sight for the blind, to release the oppressed, to proclaim the year of the Lord's favor.'

This is what is known as a "Messianic" prophecy. Jewish people in the First Century believed that God would send a "Messiah" – an "Anointed One" to save His people. The listeners in the synagogue that day would have immediately recognized Isaiah 61 as a Messianic passage. What Jesus did next, they undoubtedly did not expect. Jesus rolled up the scroll, handed it to the attendant, and returned to his seat. As everyone stared intently at him, he said, "Today this scripture is fulfilled in your hearing." The people were "amazed" at what Jesus said (Luke 4:16-22).

What was so amazing about what Jesus taught that day? He said that the scripture was "fulfilled" that day. How could it be "fulfilled" by anything other than the coming of the long-awaited Messiah? Jesus was claiming to be the Messiah – the Anointed One from God. The Spirit of the Lord "is on me." God "has anointed me." "He has sent me."

In John 5:46, Jesus told the listening crowd, "If you believed Moses, you would believe me, for he wrote about me." Luke 24:27 says that "beginning with Moses and all the prophets, he explained to them what was said in all the Scriptures concerning himself." In other words, Jesus taught that the Old Testament was pointing to him – Jesus – personally. He was claiming to be the Messiah, the Savior, sent from God.

Jesus asked his disciples from time to time who they and others thought he was. In one exchange in Matthew chapter 16, Jesus asked his disciples, "Who do people say the Son of Man [a term he used for himself] is?" They replied that the people thought he was John the Baptist, or Elijah or Jeremiah – nice compliments, but not quite right. So Jesus asked the disciples, "Who do you say I am?" Peter immediately replied "You are the Christ, the Son of the living God." "Christ" is another term for "Messiah." Jesus was pleased. Peter, who did not always get it right, got it right this time. What he got right was Jesus's identity.

In John 4:26, Jesus was talking to a Samaritan woman, who mentioned the expected coming of the Messiah. Jesus said, "I who speak to you am He." The combination of these and other passages from all four gospels shows that Jesus clearly and repeatedly claimed to be the Messiah. But what, exactly, is the Messiah?

In John chapter 8, Jesus was debating some religious leaders and said, "If anyone keeps my word, he will never see death." The response from the leaders was "Abraham died and so did the prophets, yet you say that if anyone keeps your word, he will never taste death. Are you greater than our father Abraham? He died, and so did the prophets. **Who do you think you are?**" The next volley belonged to Jesus: "Your father Abraham rejoiced at the thought of seeing my day; he saw it and was glad." The leaders were astonished by this claim: "You are not yet fifty years old. . .and you have seen Abraham!" "I tell you the truth," Jesus answered, "before Abraham was born, <u>I am</u>!"

This statement was stunningly audacious to Jewish listeners learned in the Old Testament. Jesus was unequivocally claiming to be the Messiah, and he was claiming to have existed before Abraham. Not only that, Jesus used the phrase "I am" in the first person. This was a direct reference to God's dialogue with Moses in Exodus chapter 3. Moses had heard God's voice and talked to Him. God gave Moses a message to deliver back to the people. Moses was worried that the people would not believe that Moses had really talked to God, so he asked God, "Who shall I say told me these things?" God's answer was, "I am who I am. This is what you are to say to the Israelites: 'I AM has sent me to you'" (Exodus 3:14). God does not need to identify Himself or justify His existence, He just "is." The phrase "I Am" describes the great God of the universe. Jesus was using the same phrase to describe himself. He was claiming to be God in the flesh.

This was recognized by the Jewish religious leaders, who were well familiar with Moses and Abraham. When Jesus said "I am," they "picked up stones to stone him." Their response was unambiguous. Stoning was the punishment for blasphemy. He slipped away on that occasion, but his claims to be God did not subside. In chapter 10 of the gospel of John, we read that once again, the religious leaders picked up stones to stone Jesus. He asked if he was being stoned for performing miracles. The answer: "We are not stoning you for any of these...but for blasphemy, because you, a mere man, claim to be God" (John 10:33).

These are not cherry-picked references to a few isolated instances where Jesus claimed to be God. Statements like these appear throughout the gospels. Jesus accepted worship and forgave sins (Luke 7:36-50; Mark 2:5). He claimed to have the power to judge people and grant eternal life (John 5:21-30). His teachings included the following statements about himself: (a) "I am the way, the truth and the life" (John 14:6); (b) "I am the bread of life" (John 6:35); (c) "I am the light of the world" (John 8:12); and (d) "I am the resurrection and the life" (John 11:25). He repeatedly equated himself with God by saying, for example, that to know him was to know God (John 8:19; John 14:7); to see him was to see God (John 14:9; John 12:45); to believe in him was to believe in God (John 12:44); to receive him was to receive God (Mark 9:37); to hate him was to hate God (John 15:23); and to honor him was to honor God (John 5:23).

I urge you to read the Bible for yourself and see if you notice what I noticed. Jesus spoke like no man I've ever heard. It's that quality that the people around him described as speaking "with authority." Read Matthew 4, where Jesus calls some of the disciples. He just says, "Follow me," and they immediately drop their fishing nets – their source of income – and follow him. Two of them, the brothers James and John, leave their father sitting in the boat. Read the Sermon on the Mount in Matthew chapters 5 through 7. It has an otherworldly quality. Read Matthew 9, where Jesus heals a paralyzed man. He says to the man "your sins are forgiven," and then "get up, take your mat and go home." The crowd was "awestruck." To me, when Jesus speaks, it sounds like he's speaking with the authority of God.

Rejection By Religious Leaders: Jesus came as the Messiah to the Jewish people. A Gentile woman sought Jesus's healing, and he initially refused her request, saying that he had not come for the Gentiles (Matthew 15:21-28). She persisted and Jesus, recognizing her faith, healed her even though she was a Gentile. After his death, salvation was offered universally to all mankind. While many Jewish people over the years, including today and in Jesus's day, have received Jesus as their Messiah, the Jewish religious leaders of his time rejected Jesus (John 10:31-39; 11:45-53).

Extra-Biblical Evidence

Let's revisit the statements about Jesus made by Flavius Josephus, the great Jewish historian, who wrote at the end of the First Century. Josephus wrote three passages of interest to us: one about James, the brother of Jesus, one about John the Baptist, and one about Jesus himself. We already looked at his passage about Jesus, which states that Jesus "wrought surprising feats and was a teacher of such people as accept the truth gladly." It also said that the prophets of old had "prophesied these and myriads of other marvellous things about him."

Josephus wrote the following about James:

"So he [the High Priest] called a council of the Sanhedrin and brought before them the brother of **Jesus, who was called the Christ**, whose name was James, together with some others, and having accused them of having transgressed the law, he delivered them up to be stoned" (emphasis added).[42]

Concerning John the Baptist, Josephus wrote that Herod had killed John, "though he was a good man, who bade the Jews practise virtue, be just one to another and pious toward God, and come together in baptism."[43]

Josephus corroborates many of the basic facts about Jesus: (a) his forerunner, John the Baptist, (b) his great teaching, (c) his miracles ("surprising feats"), (d) his being called the Christ, or Messiah, the fulfillment of Old Testament prophecy, and (e) his rejection by religious authorities.

That Jesus performed what appeared to be miracles is corroborated by the Second Century skeptic Celsus. Celsus asserted that Jesus acquired "magical powers" from the Egyptians. He went to Egypt and returned "highly elated at possessing these powers, and on the strength of them gave himself out to be a god."[44]

Roman writings of the time refer to the title of Jesus as Christ or "Chrestus." A letter from a father to his son in prison, in the 70s AD, refers to Jesus as the "wise king" of the Jews.[45]

We also have extra-Biblical writings of First Century Christians. Clement of Rome is mentioned in the New Testament (Philippians 4:3). He lived from 30-100 AD. He was a companion of Paul and an acquaintance of Peter, and in his writings, he confirms their martyrdom. In his first letter to the Corinthians

(AD 95),[46] Clement confirms many details of the life, death, and resurrection of Jesus. Ignatius was a student of the Apostle John and wrote around 100 AD, quoting from the New Testament. He confirms the virgin birth, deity, death, and resurrection of Jesus. He called Sunday the "Lord's day," on which worship by Christians should take place.

Archaeology provides support. For many years, the existence of Nazareth as a possible hometown of Jesus was doubted. There is a modern city of Nazareth in Galilee, but until recently there was scant evidence of a Jewish village in the Roman era. In 2009, Israeli archaeologist Yardenna Alexandre excavated archaeological remains in Nazareth that date to the time of Jesus. She told reporters, "The discovery is of the utmost importance since it reveals for the very first time a house from the Jewish village of Nazareth."[47] During Jesus's time, Nazareth had a population of around 400 and a public bath, which was important for civic and religious purposes.[48]

Analysis

There is no real dispute about any of the points in the life of Jesus except the miracles and the claim to divinity. Almost everyone acknowledges that Jesus was a great moral teacher and a good man. These are good starting points, but let's analyze the disputed points. Notice how the two disputed points are related: if Jesus was God in the flesh, would it be any wonder that he had power over nature, that he could heal people and walk on water?

Miracles

The Biblical accounts of Jesus's miracles are corroborated in part by Josephus and by the arguments of Celsus. There seems little doubt that Jesus did some things that witnesses honestly attributed to the supernatural. Were they mistaken?

Maybe Jesus was just tricking people – he didn't have the ability to work miracles, he was just a magician. I've considered that theory, but it doesn't seem to hold water. Jesus didn't have the attributes of a charlatan. He was scrupulously honest. He didn't accept rewards. He wasn't a showman. In most of the miracle accounts, he seemed to muffle all responses other than faith. He told people not to talk about the miracles.

Read the account of Jesus healing a man who was born blind in John chapter 9. Judge for yourself – does it sound like a trick? I love the story, because as a lawyer, it seems so understatedly factual. There were skeptics on the scene. They investigated, even to the point of talking to the parents of the blind man. They couldn't punch any holes in the story – the man was blind from birth, and now he could see. Jesus miraculously healed him.

Maybe the healings didn't happen at all. Maybe all of the writers who recorded the "miracles" of Jesus were just making it all up, giving false testimony – lying. This theory doesn't hang well either. The great historian Will Durant noted that the gospel writers recorded "many incidents that mere inventors would have concealed."[49] He concluded:

> "That a few simple men should in one generation have invented so powerful and appealing a personality, so lofty an ethic and so inspiring a vision of human brotherhood, would be a miracle far more incredible than any recorded in the Gospel."[50]

The ultimate fallback of those skeptical of Jesus's miracles is that they didn't happen because miracles <u>never</u>

happen. Miracles are, they assume, impossible. Natural laws are inviolable. If God exists, miracles are by definition possible because God is Himself a miracle – He transcends natural laws. He created nature and controls it. Thus, if you believe in God, it's pretty hard to also hold the belief that miracles are impossible. And if Jesus was God in the flesh, then logically he would have been capable of overriding the laws of nature. The miracles are evidence of his divinity.

Divinity

The Bible makes clear that Jesus claimed to be God and was worshiped as God. As pastor and theologian J. Sidlow Baxter has said:

> "Fundamentally, our Lord's message was Himself. He did not come merely to preach a Gospel; He himself is that Gospel. He did not come merely to give bread; He said, 'I am the bread.' He did not come merely to shed light; He said, 'I am the light.' He did not come merely to show the door; He said, 'I am the door.' He did not come merely to name a shepherd; He said, 'I am the shepherd.' He did not come merely to point the way; He said, 'I am the way, the truth, and the life.'" [51]

Let's go back to the "good teacher" point of view. How could Jesus be a "good teacher" unless the things he taught about himself are true? British author C.S. Lewis (you know him from the *Chronicles of Narnia* series) crystallized the options for us based on the teachings of Jesus:

> "A man who was merely a man and said the sort of things Jesus said would not be a great moral teacher. He would either be a lunatic – on a level

with the man who says he is a poached egg – or else he would be the Devil of Hell. You must make your choice. Either this man was, and is, the Son of God; or else a madman or something worse."[52]

Many people are surprised that Jesus claimed to be divine. Jesus was a humble servant, was he not? Yes, he was. He taught that humility is a virtue. He exhibited humility in his dealings with people. He did not want to be emperor. He washed people's feet.

Jesus displayed none of the characteristics of a mad man and he surely wasn't the "Devil of Hell." He was humble, yet claimed to be God in the flesh. Does this fit the evidence? Does it make sense? What consequences would flow from it? Let's play this out a bit.

The first words of the gospel of John are "In the beginning was the Word, and the Word was with God, and the Word was God." The word for "Word" in the original Greek is *Logos*, and it refers to an essential message from God. Later in the same passage, this "Word" is identified as Jesus. Therefore, Jesus was "with God" and "<u>was</u> God" (John 1:1). The next part is astonishing: "the Word became flesh and made his dwelling among us" (John 1:14).   Is it possible that God, in order to solve the problem of man's brokenness, took on human flesh and dwelt among His people? That He delivered a *Logos* in human form?

I once heard the following analogy. Suppose you had an anthill in your back yard, and as you watched these ants day in and day out, you grew attached to them (big supposition). One day you noticed that the anthill was in imminent danger from a predator. You wanted to warn the ants, so you yelled at them. But they didn't understand. What could you do? If you could possibly become an ant, at least temporarily, you could warn them in a way they could understand. Though this is an imperfect analogy, the point is that maybe God cared enough for us to become one of us. He "became flesh and made his dwelling among us." Jesus was that flesh.

Though we will never fully understand the concept of God taking on human flesh, there is some sense to it. What else could God do to fix man's problem? He spent hundreds of years speaking to humans through prophets. They didn't listen. He gave them rules to live by. They didn't obey them. He gave them kings and judges to lead them. They didn't follow. God couldn't get our attention, and we couldn't solve our own problem. God became one of us in order to solve the problem Himself.

Jesus interacted with people of various classes, sexes, ages, and races. Yet he seemed to concentrate on the "most broken." He healed sick people, including lepers, the lowliest outcasts of society. He traveled through Samaria and met with Samaritan people, who were viewed as a disfavored race. He elevated the status of women. He was not afraid to socialize with prostitutes, adulterers, and tax collectors – sinners – even though he was criticized for it. Though aristocrats also followed him, his chief disciples were fishermen and others of ordinary and humble means. That Jesus focused on the most broken lends support to the notion that he was God in the flesh, who came to address man's greatest spiritual need.

This makes Christianity unique among the major religions. Moses, Abraham, Mohammed, and Buddha never claimed to be God. None of the other major religions claims that God took on human flesh. This is one of the central facets of Christianity and makes it stand alone among world religions.

Other people have claimed to be divine. Several of the Roman emperors, including Nero, claimed to be gods. Some demanded worship. But the evidence belied their divinity. Nero was a rotten person. He claimed to be the incarnation of Apollo, himself a myth. Nero claimed to be a god for selfish and narcissistic reasons. None of this can be said of Jesus.

Like the virgin birth, the divinity of Jesus is one of the unique things about Christianity. Many people get it wrong; they don't understand what Jesus said about himself, or what the miracles demonstrated about him. When you put divinity and the virgin birth together, it enlightens the ubiquitous John 3:16, which states, "For God so loved the world that he gave his only begotten son..." God the heavenly Father sent His divine son to earth, and He did it out of love. If this is true, we don't have to worry that the little planet we live on in the corner of the universe is godforsaken. God entered our world, and He did it because He loves us.

8

THE DEATH OF JESUS

Everyone who knows Christians understands that the "sign" of Christianity is the cross. Christians have crosses in their churches; they wear them on necklaces, tattoo them onto their skin, and put them on bumper stickers. Why? Because their Savior, Jesus Christ, was "crucified." He was nailed to a cross and died.

That Jesus was crucified is a historical fact, essentially undoubted. There is an abundance of evidence both inside and outside the Bible.

Biblical Evidence

When Jesus was about 33 years old, after a public ministry that lasted three years, he entered the city of Jerusalem for the Jewish Passover celebration. On a Thursday night, he had his last supper with his disciples and told them that he was going to be betrayed and killed. That night, one of his disciples betrayed him with a kiss in the garden of Gethsemane, and Jesus was arrested. While in custody, he was beaten, scourged, and mocked. He was examined by the High Priests, Annas and Caiaphas, and by Herod Antipas, the administrative ruler of the Galilee region. On Friday, Jesus was sentenced by the Roman governor, Pontius Pilate, to death by crucifixion. He was taken to a hill called Golgotha or Calvary, outside the walls of the city, and nailed to a cross. Several hours later, he died, a fact that was confirmed by a Roman soldier who thrust a spear into his side. He was taken down from the cross and buried in a rock tomb in a nearby garden.

These facts are stated in the four gospels (Matthew chapters 26-27, Mark chapter 15, Luke chapters 22-23, and John chapters 13-19). Many of them are also stated in the New Testament letters, notably those of Peter and Paul, and in the book of Acts, written by Luke.

Extra-Biblical Evidence

There is abundant evidence to corroborate the Bible on the crucifixion. We have already examined a couple of weighty pieces. Tacitus, the great Roman historian, tells us that "Christus, from whom they [Christians] got their name, had been executed by sentence of the procurator Pontius Pilate when Tiberius was emperor." Tacitus also tells us that crucifixion was a common Roman form of execution: Christians in Nero's time were "nailed to crosses." Josephus, the great Jewish historian, tells us that "Pilate, upon hearing him accused by men of the highest standing among us, had condemned him to be crucified."

The British Museum has a manuscript dated shortly after 73 AD written by Mara Bar-Serapion to his son, who was in prison, to encourage him, pointing out that those who had persecuted Pythagoras, Socrates and Christ had suffered misfortune. These are not the words of a Christian, though clearly the writer wasn't antagonistic:

> "What advantage did the Athenians gain from putting Socrates to death? Famine and plague came upon them as a judgment for their crime. What advantage did the men of Samos gain from burning Pythagoras? In a moment their land was

covered with sand. <u>What advantage did the Jews gain from executing their wise King</u>? It was just after that that their kingdom was abolished. God justly avenged these three wise men: the Athenians died of hunger; the Samians were overwhelmed by the sea; the Jews, ruined and driven from their land, live in complete dispersion." (Emphasis added.)[53]

This letter, written by an independent and disinterested person, corroborates (1) Jesus's execution (2) Jesus's reputation as a wise teacher, and (3) the time of Jesus's life and death – before the Romans abolished the kingdom of the Jews, ruined their land, and drove them from it (67-73 AD.)

Archaeology has shown that crucifixion was practiced in Jerusalem in the 1st century and nails were used. One set of human remains shows a seven-inch spike through the feet with small pieces of olive wood from the cross of a 70 AD crucifixion.[54] The probable tomb that Jesus was laid in has been located. It meets the Biblical description and is dated to the First Century AD. The tomb is empty.

Pontius Pilate has been confirmed by archaeological findings. The "Pavement" near the Jaffa Gate at which Jesus was sentenced by Pilate has been located. The burial grounds of the high priest Caiaphas and his family have been found. The probable locations of the garden of Gethsemane and the upper room where the Last Supper took place have been discovered.

The "Shroud of Turin" is an interesting piece of evidence if it is genuine, but its genuineness is full of questions. It's also an interesting study in historical evidence-gathering. The Shroud is claimed to be the burial cloth of Jesus, and it contains an image of a man who was apparently crucified. The bloodstains and other marks on the cloth line up very closely with what Jesus went through. After carbon dating in the 1980s, many scholars pronounced it a fraud, but there is substantial evidence, subsequently revealed, that puts that finding in doubt.[55]

Whole books have been written about the Shroud of Turin, if you want to drill down on it. Many scholars believe the scientific evidence establishes its authenticity, and if it truly is the burial cloth of Jesus, it is a remarkable confirmation of the Biblical accounts. The debate continues, and until it is resolved with more clarity, it is too controversial and uncertain for me to include as significant evidence. We certainly don't need it on the question of Jesus's crucifixion.

Analysis

I find it reassuring, as an evidence junkie, that so much of the evidence can be observed today. You can go to Jerusalem and see the garden of Gethsemane, the little hill called Calvary, the tomb, and the locations of the Last Supper, the trials, and the sentencing of Jesus. You can walk down from the garden of Gethsemane on the Mt. of Olives into the Kidron Valley and up to the city, as the Bible describes Jesus did on the night he was betrayed. You can time how long it takes to walk from one historic location to another. The dimensions of time and topography are important elements in the gospel accounts, and you can verify them yourself.

Many details of the accounts defy the possibility of fiction. For example, the New Testament records that Jesus's body was given to a rich man named Joseph of Arimathea, a "member of the council." The "council" is the Jewish Sanhedrin, a religious ruling council. Joseph was obviously a well-known person in Jerusalem. He is mentioned nowhere else in the New Testament, but his role in connection with the crucifixion and resurrection is important: he asked Pilate for custody of Jesus's body, which was granted, and Jesus was laid in a garden tomb belonging to Joseph. Why did the New Testament writers add the detail of the identity of this person? If they were making this up, it would be disadvantageous to include a fictitious person. It would be even more risky to include someone who was well known and could be interviewed to determine whether the writings were true. The naming of Joseph of Arimathea is an indication of trustworthiness.

I find many "statements against interest" in the gospel accounts of the last hours of Jesus's life on earth. At least three New Testament authors (Matthew, John, and Peter) were disciples of Jesus and a fourth (Mark) was the "interpreter" of a disciple, Peter. The disciples are portrayed quite negatively in the accounts. Most of them ran off when Jesus was arrested. Peter, one of Jesus's closest friends, denied three times during the night that he even knew Jesus. People generally don't make themselves look bad unless they're telling the truth.

There really is no evidence against the crucifixion of Jesus under Pontius Pilate. Doubts about it are insubstantial.

We have come to a milestone point in our study. If you are open to the possibility of the supernatural, then you have a treat in store. We are going to examine the evidence for the ultimate miracle – the resurrection of Jesus. If Jesus is God, the grave cannot hold him. To the delight of evidence junkies everywhere, there is a surprising amount of evidence relating to the resurrection. Let's get to it.

9

THE RESURRECTION OF JESUS

The Bible says that Jesus died on the cross on a Friday ("Good Friday") and was buried in a sealed tomb. On Sunday, the stone sealing the entrance was found moved out of the way, and the tomb was empty. Christians believe that Jesus rose from the dead. We call this the "resurrection." We celebrate weekly by worshiping on Sundays, and we celebrate annually on a holiday popularly called "Easter" (some Christians call the holiday "Resurrection Day").

The resurrection is the "tipping point" issue of Christianity. The rise of the Christian church is recorded in the book of Acts, written by the physician, Luke. The resurrection was the foundational fact that transformed the disciples into evangelists. The gospel was spread in the early days largely through speeches by the disciples and Paul. The resurrection is the focal point of every speech.

The resurrection is <u>essential</u> to Christian faith. The apostle Paul wrote that "if Christ has not been raised, our preaching is useless and so is your faith" (1 Corinthians 15:14). John Updike, in his novel *A Prayer for Owen Meany*, says, "Anyone can be sentimental about the Nativity; any fool can feel like a Christian at Christmas. But Easter is the main event; if you don't believe in the resurrection, you're not a believer."[56]

The stakes are high. It is worth looking closely at the evidence for the resurrection.

Biblical Evidence

Jesus's body was taken down from the cross on a Friday afternoon, just before the Sabbath and the Passover celebration were to begin at sundown. Joseph of Arimathea asked Pilate for permission to take the body (Mark 15:42-47). He and a man named Nicodemus laid the body in a tomb owned by Joseph (John 19:38-42). The tomb was "cut in the rock" (Luke 23:5). Because of the impending Sabbath, there wasn't time to fully prepare the body, and the preparations could not occur during the Sabbath (sundown Friday to sundown Saturday), either. So Mary the mother of Jesus, and Mary Magdalene, took note of the location of the tomb and planned to return on Sunday to further prepare the body (Mark 15:47; Luke 53:55). In the meantime, the body was wrapped in a linen cloth with 75 pounds of spices (John 20:39-40).

The tomb was the type that could be closed off by rolling a large stone in front of the entrance, which was done (Mark 15:46). Because the religious leaders remembered that Jesus had predicted that after three days he would rise again, they asked Pilate to secure the tomb. Pilate agreed, so a seal was placed on the stone and a guard was posted (Matthew 27:62-66).

On Sunday morning, Mary the mother of Jesus, and Mary Magdalene, went to the tomb (Matthew 28:1; Luke 24:1; Mark 16:1; John 20:1). On the way, they discussed how the stone was going to be moved aside, since it was too large for them to move (Mark 16:2). When they got there, the women discovered that the stone had already been moved and the tomb was open (Mark 16:4). They went inside. The body was gone (Luke 24:3). Matthew's gospel says that they encountered an angel inside the tomb who told them that Jesus had risen (Matthew 28:2-7). They were "afraid yet filled with joy" (Matthew 28:8). They ran to tell the disciples. On the way, they encountered the risen

Jesus; they fell at his feet and worshiped him (Matthew 28:9).

The disciples did not believe the women's report at first (Luke 24:10-11). Peter and John ran to the tomb. Peter went inside and saw the strips of linen "lying by themselves" (Luke 24:12). John also saw the linens "and believed" (John 20:8).

The disciples had been cowering behind locked doors out of fear for their own safety (John 20:19). Jesus appeared to them at one of their gatherings, displaying his hands and side for them to see his wounds (John 20:20). Later, he specifically let Thomas touch the wounds, which caused the previously doubting disciple to say "my Lord and my God" (John 20:24-28). On several other occasions, Jesus talked to disciples and other followers, he ate with them, and he appeared to them (John 21; Luke 24:13-44; Acts 1:4). Jesus "appeared to more than five hundred of the brothers and sisters at the same time" (1 Corinthians 15:6). He also appeared to James, his half-brother, who was not one of the 12 disciples (1 Corinthians 15:7). Forty days after the resurrection, Jesus ascended into the clouds as the disciples watched (Luke 24:51; Acts 1:9).

The book of Acts tells us that Jesus gave his disciples "many convincing proofs that he was alive" after the resurrection (Acts 1:3).

Most of the facts about the resurrection are recorded in the gospels of Matthew, Mark, Luke, and John. However, virtually the entire New Testament testifies to the resurrection. Peter confirms it in his letters (1 Peter 1:3 and 3:21). Paul mentions it throughout his letters and builds numerous arguments around it. The book of Hebrews, the author of which is unknown (it might be Paul), mentions the resurrection twice (Hebrews 6:2 and 11:35).

The book of Acts covers a period beginning shortly after the resurrection and continuing through the ensuing 30 years as the disciples spread the news about Jesus. The resurrection is the common theme of their speeches. They were eyewitnesses, and they told people what they had seen and heard. Just a few weeks after the resurrection, Peter gave a speech in Jerusalem in which he declared, "God has raised this Jesus to life, and we are all witnesses of the fact" (Acts 2:32). Christianity grew, in the face of fierce persecution, largely on the strength of the eyewitness testimony of the resurrection.

Most of the first Christians had been raised in the Jewish faith and traditions. The Jews set aside the last day of the week, Saturday, for religious observances. However, the early Christians, after the resurrection, began to worship on Sunday instead of Saturday (Acts 20:7).

Extra-Biblical Evidence

The main piece of evidence is available for everyone to see: the empty tomb. It's there inside the Church of the Holy Sepulchre in Jerusalem. I'm not happy that people built a church over the tomb in the 4th Century, but it's there. It meets the descriptions. It has been verified historically, not to 100% certainty but to a strong probability. In the recent past, a "Garden Tomb" has been discovered outside the current Damascus Gate, and it has been floated as a possible site of the burial of Jesus. It is an outstanding place to visit, and I'm convinced that the original tomb looked very similar. The curators of the Garden Tomb don't claim that it's definitely the one; they just say it "could be." It's an interesting discussion, but here's the main point: that one is empty too. They're both empty.

A corollary to the empty tomb is the absence of a dead body, or remains of the dead body, of Jesus. Archaeology has unearthed the remains (bones) of many people who lived at the same time, including the family of High Priest Caiaphas, who was a player in the crucifixion events.[57] In the days and months following the alleged resurrection, the Romans and the Jewish religious leaders had every incentive to produce the body of Jesus and display it. That would have killed the fledgling Christian movement at its inception. There is no evidence whatsoever that anything like that happened. In modern times, extreme skeptics have proposed fanciful theories about the body of Jesus being buried in France or other places, but there is no evidence to support these theories and they appear to be profit-driven.[58]

An empty tomb, no body, no bones – this is pretty strong stuff. There's a great deal more.

We've previously looked at the writings of Jewish historian Josephus. In his passage about Jesus, he apparently wrote, "*On the third day he appeared to them restored to life.*" This sentence, in an otherwise reliable passage, is hotly contested, not because there is any evidence that Josephus didn't write it, or because some of the manuscripts of his writing don't contain it, but solely because it doesn't seem to "fit." Many scholars give good reasons for concluding that the sentence is genuine.[59] I'll leave that debate to others; I don't rely heavily on the sentence.

Josephus also describes the martyrdom of James, the brother of Jesus, which is an important brick in a wall of proof we'll examine below.

Many of the details of Roman crucifixion practices, Jewish burial practices, the identities of the players, and the locations of many of the scenes are supported by archaeology.

Vigorous persecution of Christians and the spread of Christianity are attested to in the pages of Roman writings.

We've already looked at Tacitus, the dean of Roman historians. He described the insane cruelties inflicted by Nero on Christians. He also reported on the rise of Christianity in spite of the persecution: "The pernicious superstition was checked for a short time, only to break out afresh, not only in Judea, the home of the plague, but in Rome itself." It seems ironic to think that Christianity outlasted the mighty Roman Empire and is still spreading today.

Other Roman writings corroborate the torture and execution of Christians, the spread of Christianity outwardly from Jerusalem, the high moral code of its adherents, and the worship of Jesus by early Christians. One great example is the exchange of letters between Pliny the Younger, a Roman governor, and his friend, the emperor Trajan. Pliny lived from 61 to 113 AD. In his letters, Pliny talks about how he tortured and killed Christian women who could not be made to curse Christ. The Christians "were accustomed to meet on a fixed day before dawn and sing responsively a hymn to Christ as to a god, and to bind themselves by oath, not to some crime, but not to commit fraud, theft, or adultery, not falsify their trust, nor to refuse to return a trust when called upon to do so." Pliny lamented that the Christian "superstition has spread not only to the cities but also to the villages and farms."[60]

Extra-biblical writings of First Century Christians (such as Clement and Ignatius) confirm that the resurrection was the central tenet of early Christianity.

Here's a piece of corroborating evidence that you can confirm for yourself today. Drive through any town in America and you will see at least one Christian church building with its worship service schedule on a sign outside. When do they hold their services? On Sundays. That tradition goes back to the First Century, probably to the very year of the resurrection. It was a brand new tradition then. It was a change from prior practice. Christians worship on Sundays because of the resurrection.

Analysis

As we've seen, there are quite a few "bricks" (pieces of evidence) to examine. Do they form a solid wall? Let's look at them and see if they fit together. The core facts are:

1. The grave was empty.

2. There is no record of anyone producing the dead body of Jesus.

3. Several disciples and other witnesses claimed to have seen Jesus alive; they claimed to have touched him, talked to him and eaten with him.

4. Some skeptics, like James the brother of Jesus, became believers after allegedly seeing Jesus alive.

5. Christianity grew outwardly from Jerusalem on the strength of testimony that Jesus had been raised from the dead.

6. The earliest Christians, most of whom were of Jewish upbringing, began worshiping on Sundays to commemorate the resurrection.

7. Many of the disciples and others who testified that they had seen Jesus alive after his crucifixion suffered torture and martyrdom for their beliefs.

Let's first examine these facts from the affirmative point of view – how do they provide evidence of the resurrection? Then we will look at the negative case – alternative theories that attempt to fit the facts.

Points 1 and 2 are strong pieces of evidence by themselves. They leave very little room for alternative theories.

Point 3 is strong, but not airtight. Jesus appeared to over 500 people, and 500 witnesses to anything is a lot. But why not 50,000? Why didn't he appear in a public place where a multitude could see him? Why didn't he appear to the Roman emperor, Tiberius, who could have publicized it to the world? Why did he leave any room for doubt? These questions were posed by skeptics starting with Celsus in the 2nd Century AD. There are several answers, and I'll address them in more detail in the "why" chapter below. One point about this jumps out at me.

I've written a novel, so I know something about fiction. If I were inventing the resurrection, this would have been a good place to pile on the fakery. I would have done it like this: Jesus blasts his way out of the tomb with a show of fanfare. He makes his way directly to Pilate's palace, overpowering centurions and guards to get into Pilate's bedchamber. In the Sunday morning light, Pilate jumps out of bed, grabs a sword, and starts swinging. Jesus dodges and weaves, overpowers Pilate, and grabs the sword. While holding the tip of the sword to Pilate's neck, Jesus says, "I told you, my power is greater than yours." For poetic justice, Jesus gives Pilate leprosy before he walks away. That's the way humans invent stories. I live near Hollywood.

The point is: fiction writers exaggerate, they don't understate. Putting limits on the post-resurrection appearances wouldn't have occurred to a fiction writer. According to Jewish scholar and resurrection believer Pinchas Lapide, the relatively small number of appearances is "no obstacle but rather a further proof" of the genuineness of the Biblical accounts.[61]

Point 4 – the turnaround of contemporary skeptics – is an important one for those who follow courtroom drama. Admissions obtained from hostile witnesses are often the most compelling points in a trial. We've already talked about the disciple Thomas, who was skeptical of the resurrection claims until he put his finger in Jesus's hands and side. Another interesting skeptic is James, the half-brother of Jesus. During Jesus's ministry, "even his own brothers did not believe in him" (John 7:5). After the resurrection, Jesus appeared to James (1 Corinthians 15:7). Several years later, we read that James was a "pillar" of the church in Jerusalem (Galatians 2:9). We know from Josephus that James maintained his faith until he was martyred for it. What caused this turnaround in James? The physical evidence – he saw the risen Jesus.

Point 5 is that the fledgling movement started in the same city where the crucifixion and burial took place. It grew based on speeches by the disciples, like Peter's speech in Acts chapter 2, given in Jerusalem about seven weeks after the crucifixion, in which he emphasized the fact that Jesus had been raised to life, which he personally witnessed. Producing a dead body would have thoroughly rebutted Peter's speech, and instead of thousands of people being added to the church, the movement would have stopped right there. The Romans and the Jewish religious leaders opposed the rise of Christianity from the beginning. Displaying the dead body of Jesus – either inside or outside the tomb – would have nipped Christianity in the bud.

Point 6 is highly significant. Christianity changed long-held social customs, such as worship on Saturday (which virtually all early Christians were used to doing, having been raised as Jews). There must have been a dramatic change-inducing event that caused this. As C.F.D. Moule of Cambridge University has stated, the emergence of the church "rips a hole in history, a hole the size and shape of the Resurrection."[62]

Point 7 is also crucial. Every person who wrote about the resurrection, every person who witnessed Jesus alive after the crucifixion, and everyone who believed in the resurrection was a candidate for intense persecution. Except John, who survived torture, all of the New Testament writers were likely martyred. Why would someone make up stories that would bring about torture or execution for himself and his family? The New Testament accounts of the resurrection must be credited as "statements against interest," and therefore endued with trustworthiness.

In my practice as a courtroom lawyer, I often see cases that turn on one witness's testimony or a key document. In those situations, I look for internal "badges of truth." Is there internal consistency? Did the witness or writer have an incentive to report truthfully? Has she said something against her self-interest? Is there something unusual or unexpected in the report that wouldn't be in there unless the writer was telling the truth? As I look at the Biblical accounts of the resurrection, I find some of these things. I don't find any red flags.

The Bible includes four factual accounts of the resurrection, plus additional writings from purported eyewitnesses (like Peter). The fact that all four gospel writers report that Jesus was raised from the dead lends credence to the event. If it had not happened, you might expect at least one of the biographers not to mention it. The accounts all corroborate each other in the major details – Jesus was crucified on a Friday; he was laid in the tomb of a rich man in a garden; some of his family and followers came on Sunday morning to prepare his body for long-term burial; they discovered that the tomb was empty; they encountered the risen Jesus; and in the ensuing days, Jesus had repeated encounters with many witnesses, encounters that included touching, talking and eating.

The four gospel accounts contain some apparent minor differences, and some opponents have offered this as evidence of fabrication, but it actually bolsters their credibility. All of the differences relate to minor details, like the time of day when the first of his followers approached the tomb on Sunday morning, how many women were present, etc.[63] Some details are present in one account and missing in others. There are good explanations for these minor differences. More important, the fact that the four accounts do not track each other verbatim is another indication of truthfulness. Fabricators would agree on the story among themselves and set it out identically, using canned phrases. Nothing of the sort appears in the gospel accounts of the resurrection.

One extraordinary detail is that all four gospels record that the empty tomb was discovered by women. No one would make this up. Women in the First Century were on a low rung of the social ladder. An old rabbinical saying was "let the words of the Law be burned rather than delivered to a woman." Women's testimony was regarded as worthless and women were not allowed to serve as legal witnesses.[64] Things are quite different today. The testimony of women is just as valid and credible as the testimony of men. But no First Century writer would include such a detail unless it were true. It is, in essence, a statement against interest that supports the fact that the writers were endeavoring to be truthful.

There are two key details of the crucifixion-resurrection accounts that the Bible writers observed but did not understand: Jesus' sweating of blood the night he was betrayed, and the flow of blood and water from Jesus when the Roman soldier pushed his spear into Jesus's side after he died on the cross. It is likely that none of the writers had ever encountered these phenomena before, and it is certain that they did not understand the medical phenomena at play. Thus, it is unlikely that they would have made these things up. Modern medical knowledge confirms that a person can literally sweat blood – it is a medical condition called hematidrosis. It is not very common, but it is associated with a high degree of psychological stress. Severe anxiety causes the release of chemicals that break down the capillaries in the sweat glands. A small amount of blood enters the glands, and the sweat comes out tinged with blood. With respect to the blood and water that flowed out of Jesus's side, what happened is this: hypovolemic shock (a state of decreased blood volume caused by hemorrhaging or dehydration) caused a rapid heart rate and eventually heart failure. This caused an excess of fluid around the heart (pericardial effusion) and the lungs (pleural effusion). This fluid (clear, like water) is what came out, along with blood, when the spear was thrust in. Doctors today understand these phenomena, but the New Testament writers did not. They simply recorded what they saw or what eyewitnesses reported.

In summary, the affirmative case for the resurrection is quite strong. It happened a long time ago and some of the evidence is gone, but as Professor Thomas Arnold, chairman of the history department at Oxford University, has said, "I have been used for many years to study the histories of other times, and to examine and weigh the evidence of those who have written about them, and I know of no one fact in the history of mankind which is proved by better and fuller evidence of every sort, than the great sign which God has given us that Christ died and rose again from the dead."[65]

The Biblical writings are from competent witnesses and investigators, and they contain badges of truth. Significant corroboration exists outside the central writings. We'll now look at the alternative theories and see how strong they are.

The Opposing Case

If there are two sides to every story, the weakness of one side strengthens the other side. Every good trial lawyer knows this. In three decades of trying cases, I've found that my case is usually won when the other side brings its evidence. Why? Because of "cross-examination" (apt name, isn't it?). When the other guy's case is weak, I will expose the weaknesses through his own witnesses and documents. I will obtain damaging admissions from his experts.

The resurrection is an event that either happened or it didn't happen. We have looked at the evidence that it happened, and the evidence looks solid. Now, let's look at the other side's case.

Theories That Assume Intentional Deception

Stolen Body: The original argument, recorded in the Bible itself, was that the disciples stole the body (Matthew 28:11-15). This argument is extremely weak. In the wake of Jesus's arrest, torture, and crucifixion, the disciples were cowering behind locked doors (John 20:19). They naturally thought they were next in line. To pull off the bold move of stealing the body from a sealed tomb under armed guard was beyond their capabilities and character. Even if they had, the next problem is equally severe. They would have had to hide the body quickly and permanently in a way that would leave no trace forever. The Romans and Jewish religious leaders had every incentive and every power to uncover such a fraud and find the body. Again, the notion that the disciples had the requisite character and skill to pull this off is dubious. Finally, the next problem is the most insurmountable of all. All 11 disciples and their colleagues would have had to keep this secret to the end of their lives and go to their deaths for something they knew was a lie. It is nearly impossible to imagine any 11 people being able to do this. <u>These 11 were known to be both scrupulously honest</u> – the disciples of an honest and humble man – and in a state of cowardice after the crucifixion.[66]

If the authorities truly believed that the disciples stole the body, if there had been any evidence of that, they would surely have imprisoned and probably executed them for the crime. The book of Acts records that a few weeks after the resurrection, the disciples Peter and John entered the Temple courts in Jerusalem and were arrested by the Temple guard. They were brought before the Sanhedrin, the Jewish ruling council that had ordered Jesus's death. The charge was that Peter and John had healed a lame man "in the name of Jesus." The Sanhedrin ordered them to stop speaking in the name of Jesus, and set them free. (See Acts chapters 3 and 4.) There is no way the Sanhedrin would have let Peter and John go free if there was any serious claim that they had stolen Jesus's dead body. Thus, the Sanhedrin had undoubtedly, by this time, rejected or abandoned any claim that the disciples had stolen the body.

One thing lawyers know about conspiracies is that the agreed-upon story quickly shows signs of manufacture or inconsistency. It doesn't take long before someone "cracks" to save his skin.

Charles Colson saw this in the Watergate conspiracy. Watergate was one of the biggest political scandals in U.S. history, resulting in the impeachment and resignation of President Nixon. The scandal involved illegal activities of the Nixon Administration directed toward political rivals. Colson was the White House Counsel, sometimes referred to as the "hatchet man." The cover-up involved Colson and several other highly intelligent men in extremely powerful positions, intensely loyal to the president. They agreed on a story and began a program of lies and obfuscation. It took two weeks for one key conspirator to turn state's evidence, and "then everybody else jumped ship in order to save themselves."[67]

Conspiracies of any sort are almost impossible to hold together long. When a large number of people are involved, and the consequence is torture and death, it is inconceivable that a conspiracy can be maintained for decades. As Colson, a self-described "expert in cover-ups," says, "Nothing less than a resurrected Christ could have caused those men to maintain to their dying whispers that Jesus is alive and is Lord."[68]

There is no evidence anywhere that the disciples were anything other than men of the highest integrity, committed to the truth. It is against human nature for people to die for something they know is a lie. William Lane Craig, a Christian philosopher who has debated numerous atheists and other skeptics, says that no one today seriously espouses the theory that the disciples stole the body.[69] It is not doubted that the disciples sincerely believed the truth of the resurrection, which they proclaimed to their deaths. This is utterly inconsistent with the conspiracy theory.

I have a lot of experience in ferreting out lies. My job as a lawyer makes me an officer of the court, with an obligation both to tell the truth and to bring out the truth in a case. Over the course of my career, I've become pretty good, I think, at seeing the telltale signs of lies. Inconsistencies in a witness's story become apparent. Documents undercut the story. Physical facts don't fit. Then when the pressure is applied, the lie is usually exposed.

All of those methods were available in the First Century to test the Biblical accounts. Physical evidence and numerous eyewitnesses were available to undercut them if they were lying. The writers were subjected to pressure that makes cross-examination pale in comparison. The story held. It holds to this day.

The theory that the disciples stole the body, hid it, lied about it, and suffered martyrdom for the lie is beyond far-fetched. No rational person undertaking a serious analysis would believe it. It would require far more faith than to believe in the resurrection.

Metaphorical Rise: Some people have suggested that the New Testament writers are not describing a physical resurrection of Jesus, just that he lived on in spirit or in his teachings. This is a corollary to the stolen body theory and suffers from the same problems.

In no way can it fairly be said that the writers are describing a non-physical resurrection. This is the very point of the description of Doubting Thomas. He wouldn't believe until he put his fingers in the wounds. He touched the wounds and believed. The events make no sense if the resurrection was metaphorical.

All of the accounts of the resurrection appeal to what the witnesses sensed – what they saw, what they heard, what they felt with their fingers. Jesus walked, he spoke, he ate. These are not things you would say about someone who was only with you "in spirit." The writers seem intentionally to have included these details in order to portray that the resurrection was physical.

The grave was empty – all four gospel writers say so. The authorities could have nipped Christianity in the bud, and had every incentive to do so, by producing the body if the resurrection was simply "in spirit." What would have been the point of changing the day of worship to Sunday if nothing actually happened that day?

Thus, the "metaphorical rise" theory falls squarely within the intentional deception category. If Jesus only rose metaphorically, the writers were lying about it because they described a physical resurrection. Those same people who lied about it went to their deaths for the sake of the alleged lie. The theory has gaping holes.

Later Invention: To get around the conspiracy obstacles, some skeptics have proposed that the accounts of the resurrection were not written by the disciples or their contemporaries, but were rather composed a century later, after the disciples and the witnesses were dead. The writers, whoever they were, fabricated the resurrection for religious propaganda purposes. This theory only solves some of the problems of the stolen-body theory, and creates a host of new ones. It does not overcome the problems of the empty grave, the absence of a body, the rise of the church from the alleged location of the resurrection, and the radical change in social customs.

The new problems brought by the "later invention" theory start with the fact that there is no positive evidence in its favor. If the gospels weren't written by contemporaries, then who wrote them? No plausible authors have been identified. No circumstances surrounding the alleged late authorship have come to light. The only asserted "evidence" is actually a lack of evidence – for three of the four gospels, the earliest manuscripts are dated well into the Second Century AD. But gaps between original writing and earliest manuscripts are common with ancient texts. The gap here is actually very small, and is explained by the fire in Rome, the destruction of Jerusalem, and both religious and civil persecution of Christians. The manuscript evidence for the Bible is quite rich compared to other ancient writings. Indeed, the "later invention" theory took a major hit with the discovery that the gospel of John was copied in Egypt 30 years after it was written.

But the later invention theory is demolished by the fact that the first writings about the resurrection were the letters of Paul, not the gospels. The general timing of Paul's writings is not doubted; he wrote his epistles from the 40s to the 60s AD, when he was martyred. He wrote when the evidence was fresh and the witnesses were still alive. He also incorporated the oral "creed" that had been told and retold concerning the resurrection since the early days:

> "For what I received I passed on to you as of first importance: that Christ died for our sins according to the Scriptures, that he was buried, that he was raised on the third day according to the Scriptures, and that he appeared to Peter, and then to the Twelve. After that, he appeared to more than five hundred of the brothers at the same time, most of whom are still living, though some have fallen asleep. Then he appeared to James, then to all the apostles, and last of all he appeared to me also . . ." (1 Corinthians 15:3-8).

Thus, the resurrection, if it was "invented," was the invention of the eyewitnesses themselves, and their contemporaries, not a far-removed generation.

The "later invention" theory has difficulty dealing with the fact that whoever "invented" the resurrection was lying in order to deceive people. Because there were multiple authors, there would have had to be a conspiracy. The books would have had to be written at around the same time by people who knew each other. There is simply no evidence for this. All of the conspiracy problems remain.

If the gospels were written, as the "later invention" theory suggests, after 150 AD, then how do we explain the meteoric rise of the church, in the face of intense persecution, in the previous 120 years? How do we explain worship on Sundays before that time? The holes are just too big and numerous to fill.

Are the deception theories possible? Maybe. Are they plausible? No.

Theories That Assume a Grand Mistake

There have been suggestions over the years that the New Testament writers, and/or the witnesses whose testimony they rely on, were sincerely "mistaken" about the resurrection. The theories include (a) mass hallucination, (b) Jesus did not really die on the cross but "swooned," and revived in the tomb, (c) a third party stole the dead body of Jesus, leaving an empty tomb, and (d) the women and disciples simply went to the wrong tomb.

The Hallucination Theory: This theory contends that the persons who claimed to have seen Jesus alive really only saw hallucinations. They were so filled with religious fervor or hopeful optimism, that they imagined they saw a risen Jesus. Let's look at the evidence.

The idea that more than 500 people can see the same hallucination has been debunked by hallucination experts. According to Gary Collins, Ph.D., former chairman of the psychology department at Trinity Evangelical Divinity School, "[h]allucinations are individual occurrences. By their very nature, only one person can see a given hallucination at a time. . . . Neither is it possible that one person could somehow induce an hallucination in somebody else."[70] In addition, James and Thomas were skeptics, and therefore not good candidates for hallucinations. Nor were the fearful, doubtful, despairing disciples, in the wake of the crucifixion, so full of religious fervor that they were likely to hallucinate. Hallucinations are very rare. It simply is not believable that over the course of many weeks, people from all sorts of backgrounds and in all sorts of places experienced the same hallucination.

The hallucination theory fails to account for the fact that the gospels and Acts say repeatedly that the post-resurrection encounters with Jesus involved more than merely "seeing" him. The witnesses say they talked to him, walked with him, ate with him and touched him. These accounts are deliberate falsehoods if the witnesses merely suffered hallucinations. Thus, the attractiveness of the theory – its apparent explanation for the disciples' sincerity in preaching the resurrection and their willingness to suffer torture and death for their belief in it – dissolves upon close inspection.

Finally, the hallucination theory does not explain the empty tomb and the missing body. Opponents of Christianity in the early days could have snuffed it out by opening the tomb or producing the body. The hallucination theory cannot stand alone; it must be combined with, for example, the stolen body theory with all of its own insurmountable problems. The problems multiply.

The hallucination theory does not fit the evidence and has few adherents.

The Swoon Theory: The swoon theory suggests that Jesus was not really dead when he was taken down from the cross. He had merely fainted or was in a swoon. After being placed in the tomb, the cool air revived him. He somehow got out of the tomb and appeared alive to many people. They genuinely thought he had been resurrected from the dead. Jesus either told people that he had been dead, or let others believe that he had been. This theory cannot be found anywhere before the 20th Century. In the 1970s, the swoon theory was the subject of a book called *The Passion Play*.

The swoon theory has been described by theologian Luke Timothy Johnson as "the purest poppycock, the product of fevered imagination rather than careful analysis."[71] There are so many problems with the theory that it has gained virtually no following. Problems dog the theory at every step: Jesus was unquestionably dead on the cross; even if he were not dead, he could not possibly have revived in the tomb; even if he had revived, he could never have unwrapped himself from the grave clothes, entwined with 75 pounds of spices; he could never have opened the tomb from the inside (rolling aside a large stone designed to be opened only by several healthy men from the outside) or walked out in his condition (with gaping wounds in his feet); and even if all this had happened, he would have been wounded, starving, dehydrated and barely alive – not the type of figure that could convince anyone that he had conquered death.

Aside from these physical and medical problems, there is the psychological problem of presuming that the man who brought the world the greatest ethical teaching it has ever known, who taught truth and loved his disciples, this same man deceived his disciples into believing he had risen from the dead, knowing they would go to their deaths for believing it. According to the Bible, Jesus predicted his resurrection before his death (John 2:18-21; Matthew 12:38-40), and after he arose, he announced it to his disciples. If he did not in fact die, he was lying.

Let's examine the evidence on the threshold issue – whether Jesus was really dead when he was taken down from the cross. To examine Jesus' medical condition, we start with the flogging that the Bible says was ordered by Pilate (Mark 15:15) and would have been common for someone sentenced to crucifixion. In this flogging, a Roman soldier used a whip of braided leather thongs with metal balls woven into them. The balls would cause deep bruising. The whip also had pieces of sharp bone that could cut into the flesh. The victim's back would be shredded so that part of the spine was sometimes exposed by the deep cuts. Lacerations would tear into the skeletal muscles. Some victims actually died before the crucifixion. Many flogging victims would go into hypovolemic shock from the loss of blood. Dr. Alexander Metherell describes the medical effects: "First, the heart races to try to pump blood that isn't there; second, the blood pressure drops, causing fainting or collapse; third, the kidneys stop producing urine to maintain what volume of blood is left; fourth, the person becomes very thirsty and the body craves fluids to replace the lost blood volume."[72]

Next came the journey to the crucifixion site, followed by the crucifixion itself. The pain of crucifixion was unbearable – beyond words to describe, so a new word was invented: *excruciating*, which literally means "out of the cross." Crucifixion involves stretching the arms and dislocating both shoulders. As Dr. Metherell describes it, "[o]nce a person is hanging in the vertical position, crucifixion is essentially an agonizingly slow death by asphyxiation."[73] The stresses on the muscles and diaphragm put the chest into the inhaled position, so in order to exhale, the person must push up on his feet. The nail(s) would then tear through the feet, eventually locking on the tarsal bones. The victim died when he was physically unable to push up to breathe.

The gospel of John reports that a Roman soldier thrust a spear in Jesus's side to test whether he was dead. A mixture of blood and water came out (John 19:34). The writer, John, actually observed this (John 19:35). He wasn't trained in medicine and couldn't have known what it meant. It clearly meant that Jesus was dead. The clear fluid evinced hypovolemic shock, which led to pericardial effusion, which resulted in heart failure. If Jesus had not been dead, blood would have spurted out with each heartbeat. The Roman soldier also knew what the clear fluid meant, though he didn't understand the science. If he had not seen the clear fluid, he would have broken Jesus's legs to ensure a quick death (John 19:33), but the clear fluid told him he didn't need to.

The Romans were experts at killing people. They would not have made a mistake about Jesus being dead.

In an article in the *Journal of the American Medical Association* entitled "On the Physical Death of Jesus Christ," Drs. William E. Edwards and colleagues report that like most crucifixion victims, Jesus died of "hypovolemic shock and exhaustion asphyxia." Dr. Edwards, of the Mayo Clinic, concludes: "Clearly, the weight of the historical and medical evidence indicates that Jesus was dead before the wound to his side was inflicted . . . Accordingly, interpretations based on the assumption that Jesus did not die on the cross appear to be at odds with modern medical knowledge."[74]

Jesus could not have survived the ordeal of flogging followed by crucifixion. The swoon theory is "impossible," according to Dr. Metherell.[75]

There is a final problem. If Jesus did not rise from the dead, but merely revived after a swoon, he would have had to die for real, eventually. There would have been a corpse. The missing body is a perpetual problem that is not solved by the swoon theory.

The Stolen Body (Third Party) Theory: Another theory proposes that Jesus truly died, but his body was stolen and hidden by someone other than the disciples. Notice that this theory acknowledges the true death of Jesus, the empty tomb and the missing body. According to the gospel of John, this was Mary Magdalene's first assumption upon finding the tomb empty. She saw a man outside the tomb and thought it was the "gardener," who had carried the body away. She asked the man where he had put the body so that she could go there. But the man was not the gardener – it was Jesus himself. Mary knew his voice. When he said "Mary," she recognized him.

The notion that a well-intentioned gardener moved the body could not possibly be true. The tomb was guarded and sealed. There would have been no reason for a gardener to move the body on the Sabbath. If he had done so, then the body could still have been found and displayed. If the dead body was simply moved, how could Jesus appear alive to more than 500 people?

Maybe a third party stole the body, intending to make it falsely appear that Jesus had been raised from the dead. There are some major problems with this theory. It runs up against: (1) the guards at the tomb; (2) the fact that if someone had really stolen the body, he (or they) would surely have been imprisoned and probably executed for the crime; (3) the body would likely have been recovered and displayed, thus eradicating Christianity; (4) Jesus was seen alive after the crucifixion by the disciples and more than 500 other people; and (5) perhaps most significant, the disciples and others went to their deaths proclaiming that they were eyewitnesses to the risen Jesus. It wasn't just the empty tomb but the fact that they had seen him, heard him, and touched him. If they knew that he had not arisen, then they were proclaiming, and dying for, a lie.

The Wrong Tomb Theory: In 1907, a man named Kirsopp Lake proposed that the women who discovered the empty tomb simply went to the wrong one. According to this theory, Jesus really died, and the belief in the empty tomb was genuine but mistaken. This theory never generated a following. The Bible says that when Jesus was laid in the tomb, Mary "gazed" at the tomb, undoubtedly because she intended to return after the Sabbath, and wanted to mark its location (Mark 15:47). Several other people observed the empty tomb, and it is not likely that all were mistaken about its location. Joseph of Arimathea owned the tomb, and could have been consulted about the location of the "right" tomb. Nicodemus knew where the right tomb was. Both Joseph and Nicodemus were members of the Sanhedrin, and the Sanhedrin unquestionably "knew where they lived." It behooved the authorities to find and produce the body to rebut the disciples' teaching about the resurrection. If there was any merit to the contention that the body was just lost, an exhaustive search would have been made and the body produced. Finally, the disciples' and the gospels' testimony is not restricted to the empty grave. More than 500 persons are said to have seen Jesus alive, talked to him, eaten with him, walked with him and even touched him. Those statements would all be intentional falsehoods if in fact the arguments about the resurrection were based solely on the empty tomb. The "wrong tomb" theory has no merit.

Addressing the "mistaken disciples" theories, Dr. William Lane Craig has said:

> "Again, I want to emphasize that scarcely any modern historian or biblical critic would hold to these theories. They are almost completely passé. You may say to yourselves at this point, 'Well, then, what explanation of the empty tomb do modern critics offer who deny the resurrection?'

The fact is that they are self-confessedly without any explanation to offer. There simply is no plausible natural explanation available today to account for how Jesus' tomb became empty. If we deny the resurrection of Jesus, we are left with an inexplicable mystery."[76]

Summary: These are all the theories that have been posed in 2,000 years.[77] Every one of them has gaping flaws. If one open-mindedly examines the evidence and compares the competing theories, the one that makes the most sense – the only one that makes any sense at all – is that Jesus truly died and then truly rose from the dead. As Pinchas Lapide,[78] the late New Testament scholar at Hebrew University (and not a Christian) says:

> "If the defeated and depressed group of disciples overnight could change into a victorious movement of faith, based only on autosuggestion or self-deception ... then this would be a much greater miracle than the resurrection itself."[79]

It is significant that there are so many theories that attempt to explain the empty tomb. The emptiness of the tomb is almost universally acknowledged. William Lane Craig can name 44 scholars of all backgrounds – Catholic, Protestant and Jewish, liberal and conservative – that acknowledge that the tomb was empty.[80] The alternative theories that attempt to explain the empty tomb tend to ignore the substantial additional evidence of the resurrection.

Ultimately, all of the opposition theories bump up against the plain, observable facts. The empty tomb is still empty today. Christianity grew into a mass, worldwide movement. The disciples and other witnesses held tenaciously to their belief in the resurrection in the face of persecution and death. Only a true, bodily resurrection explains these facts.

I have thoroughly examined the evidence for and against the resurrection as an experienced trial lawyer. My analysis is that the affirmative case is strong, while the opposing theories are weak. Only one theory can be true, and in my opinion, as an expert at analyzing evidence, the actual, physical resurrection of Jesus is the true explanation. The palpable weakness of the opposing theories only strengthens the case for the resurrection.

Taking my lawyer hat off, analyzing the evidence as a member of the human race, I fully accept the challenge laid out at the beginning of this chapter. If the resurrection is a lie, then my faith is useless. However, if it happened, it rips a hole in history. I believe it happened. It has changed my life.

10

EXPERIENTIAL EVIDENCE

I mentioned earlier that I'm a competitive swimmer, and when a new training theory or piece of equipment comes along, I like to try it out and see if it works for me. The proof is in the pudding. I also mentioned that what got me interested in Jesus in the first place was that I had friends who were believers, and it clearly made a difference in their lives. If Jesus is divine, then the people who have him in their lives ought to reflect his divinity in some way. The genuine experiences of believers in the trenches are "evidence" worth examining.

In my case, because I have walked with Jesus for 40 years now, I can "testify" as a "witness." He's real. I interact with him on a daily basis. I see and feel his influence all around and inside me. Thoughts come into my head that have his signature voice.

Jesus has changed my life. I don't have one of those dramatic life-change stories, as if Jesus had saved me from the depths of alcoholism or drug addiction. I know people who've had that experience, and it's good evidence too. My changes have been more internal. He changed my view of the world, my passions, and my purpose in life. I've had prayers answered. I've seen and experienced things that can only be attributed to divine influence. It works for me.

"It works for me" sounds subjective and conclusory. What exactly, you might ask, "works?" Let me share a couple of things.

I now realize that my life has a purpose and meaning. Before I became a Christian, I was always looking for this. God Himself created this yearning inside of us – the Bible says that God has "set eternity in the hearts of men" (Ecclesiastes 3:11). A sense of eternity was certainly in my heart and I can tell you that finding my purpose has changed everything about my life. It gives me an anchor, a compass. It gives me peace and pushes me to think beyond myself.

The Bible says that God created people in His "image." I didn't know what that meant for a long time. I still don't understand it completely but I do know this: God is a God of grace, forgiveness, and sacrificial love. I was born to be like that. It's hard to do, but seeing that it's what I'm <u>supposed</u> to do makes sense to me. It aligns.

I sense truth and beauty, and I appreciate them now that I know that they're real, and where they come from. I have a heightened sense for the non-material reality of life.

I have brothers and sisters in Kenya. I wasn't prepared for this aspect of Christianity. Because of what Jesus did, all his followers are part of God's "family." I'm involved in a ministry that takes me to Kenya – specifically, into the heart of the infamous slums of Nairobi. I work arm and arm with Kenyans. There was an instant bond when I met them. They're truly my brothers and sisters, even though we're as different on the outside as people can be. I can't explain this without Jesus.

Another thing that works for me is the Bible. I've now studied it for 40 years, including taking seminary classes. I've lived by its principles as best I can. I've had doubts and questions but my admiration for the Bible has only increased. There's a cohesiveness in it, a depth that surpasses human knowledge. A lot of people don't understand the Bible and make gross errors based on what they think it says. I've gone deep and I think I understand it pretty well. The nuances create an awe in me. The Sermon on the Mount, the most famous address of Jesus, has a "rightness" about it just like Beethoven's music.

I'm well aware that there are millions of "Christians" who talk the talk but don't walk the walk. A skeptic might point to them and say, "See, it doesn't work." The answer is that to see life change in a person, the person himself must cooperate. He must have "faith." Weak or non-genuine Christians are lacking here. The fact remains that the power of Jesus has manifested itself in and through a multitude of people through the ages. If you're interested in this type of evidence, as I was, talk to people who are genuine Christians about their faith.

Let me give you some examples. One of my Christian heroes is William Wilberforce, a British politician who lived from 1759 to 1833. Like me, Wilberforce had some Christian influence early in his life but did not become a follower of Jesus until he was an adult. It changed him powerfully. Already a Member of Parliament, he thought about quitting politics to go into ministry. Instead, he concluded that God had called him to stay in Parliament and fight for just causes. He chose a big one – the abolition of the slave trade, one of the greatest evils the world has ever seen. His cause was unpopular when he began. His work took decades to complete. However, in 1807 England abolished the slave trade, and in 1833, days before Wilberforce died, it abolished slavery altogether. The legislation was driven by Wilberforce, who in turn was driven by his faith in Jesus. For him, for England, and for millions of people saved from slavery, it "worked."

Abraham Lincoln and Martin Luther King, Jr. were two of the greatest forces for equality in the United States. Lincoln not only freed the slaves in the US, he presided over a civil war to hold the country together. It was probably the hardest job ever given to a President, and he is now regarded as our greatest President. Lincoln was an agnostic until he reached the age of 40. Then he read a book called *The Christian's Defence* by Dr. James Smith, which discussed the historical reality of the events in Jesus's life. The evidence in the book convinced Lincoln "of the truth of the Christian religion."[81] Lincoln gave some of the greatest speeches ever given. Read Lincoln's Second Inaugural Address and you will see Biblical principles laced throughout it. He was guided by those principles in freeing the slaves and fighting the Great War.

Martin Luther King, Jr. was, of course, a "Reverend" – a Christian minister. He was the leader of the US civil rights movement in the 1950s and 1960s. Where did his lofty principles of equality, freedom, loving enemies, and non-violence come from? "All men, created alike in the image of God, are inseparably bound together," King wrote in 1956. "This is at the very heart of the Christian gospel."[82] When he was accused of being an "extremist," King referred to Jesus's Sermon on the Mount as an appeal to "extreme" love ("love your enemies") and Jesus as an "extremist for love" in going to the cross.[83]

"That's history," you may say. "Have you got any modern examples? People you actually know?" I do. I have so many that I have to be selective. Here are two:

A few years ago, I was invited to speak in the chapel at the New Tribes Mission training center. The people who go to that training center aren't missionaries yet, but they want to be. They go there to be trained in other cultures. After I spoke in the chapel, I wandered into a classroom where a seasoned missionary was teaching about animism, a common and dangerous belief system among native tribes in remote parts of the world. Here's what blew me away: three mothers with infants standing in the back of the classroom holding their babies. Young American couples were about to start their families and raise their kids in jungles. Can you imagine the commitment? What could explain such a phenomenon? I can't, not without Jesus.

Months later, I went to the jungle myself, just for a visit. I was flown in a 2-seat plane that landed on a grass strip on the side of a mountain in Papua New Guinea. I spent the day there. I talked to a local man who told the story of the village from the time before the people there were introduced to Jesus. It was a common story. Invariably, a child would die from a disease. Someone with supposed knowledge of the spirit world would accuse a person in the village – always a woman – of being a witch. The child died because of the witch. The "witch" would then be burned alive. This scene would be played out every few years in village after village. Everyone lived in fear of spirits that had to be appeased. Every time a child died, a woman would be blamed and lose her life.

Jesus broke the chain in that village. He broke the fear. He broke the killings. He even broke the cycle of death from disease. The villagers had been in bondage to their superstitions and he brought freedom. To the village of Dinangat in Papua New Guinea, it "works."

I could go on, but you get the point. It's easy to look at nominal Christians who don't follow true Biblical principles and say "it doesn't work." I agree. It doesn't work unless you really give it a go. Lots and lots of people have given it a go, and it has worked for them. I count myself among them.

11

"WHY?" – QUESTIONS BEHIND THE EVIDENCE

I've spent many years litigating cases involving pharmaceuticals – drugs and medicines. I'm personally fascinated by how drugs work. Quite a bit of the evidence in the pharmaceutical world comes from statistical or "observational" studies, while the gold standard is the clinical trial where one group gets the study drug and the other gets a placebo. Studies produce tons of evidence, but the literature is filled with studies that got it wrong. A single study proves nothing, and you can get the wrong result even with a hundred studies.

How do you ensure that the studies are giving you the right result? I found myself incessantly asking the question: why? Why did this study produce the reported result? Was it a true measure of the drug's effects? Or was it driven by one of the many forms of bias? Was it skewed, i.e. not a true test? Why does the drug appear to be efficacious? Is there a plausible mechanism of action behind it? Why does it apparently produce side effects in the kidney? What exactly is going on in the kidney when the drug is in the bloodstream?

The "why" questions help ferret out bad evidence. They can also help supply the glue that fits the pieces of "hard" evidence together.

We risk crossing from evidence to philosophy here, so I won't spend much time on it. I'd like to examine the "why" questions relating to Jesus so we can put the evidence into proper perspective.

Why did Jesus have to die?

The evidence is clear that Jesus was crucified, and that this is fundamental to the Christian faith. If Jesus were merely a good moral teacher, he wouldn't have had to die. But the Bible teaches that Jesus <u>had</u> to die. It was his <u>mission</u>. He said so himself. Why, then, did he have to die?

The Bible teaches the sacrificial nature of Jesus's death. Jesus said "The good shepherd lays down his life for the sheep… The reason my Father loves me is that I lay down my life – only to take it up again. No one takes it from me, but I lay it down of my own accord" (John 10: 11, 17-18). In other words, Jesus came to die – it was his ultimate mission – and his death was "for the sheep." It was to benefit us. "But God demonstrates his own love for us in this: While we were still sinners, Christ died <u>for us</u>" (Romans 5:8).

The death of Jesus was a <u>payment</u> for man's "sins." The original Greek word for sin means missing the mark, like shooting an arrow and missing the target. It means that every person has fallen short or become broken in some respect. You might be able to observe this yourself. Is there sin in the world? Is society broken? Pick up a newspaper or listen to country music and you won't be able to miss it.

Maybe you have personally experienced the brokenness. I'm not throwing stones; I'm as guilty as the next person. It affects everyone. The main point is this: God devised a solution for the brokenness, and it's Jesus. He paid the penalty for sin.

According to the most famous verse in the Bible, John 3:16, God "gave" his one and only Son, Jesus, because he "so loved the world." Jesus paid for our sin with his life. Jesus "gave himself for a ransom" (1 Timothy 2:6). God "sent his Son as an atoning sacrifice for our sins" (1 John 4:10). "Christ was sacrificed once to take away the sins of many people" (Hebrews 9:28).

Because of what Jesus did, a person's sins can be <u>forgiven</u>. "We have redemption through his blood, the forgiveness of sins, in accordance with the riches of God's grace" (Ephesians 1:7). My sin created a rift in the relationship between God and me. Forgiveness restores the relationship. God "reconciled us to himself through Christ" (2 Corinthians 5:18).

Did you ever notice how so many churches have the word "Grace" in their names? Did you notice how the most famous Christian hymn is called "Amazing Grace?" What's the deal with grace? Grace is God's favor, bestowed without merit. No Christian can boast that he "earned" God's favor. He got it for free. Well, a huge price was paid, but it was paid by Jesus, not by me. Thus, many of the people who get Christianity "wrong" think that their faith makes them special, or holier than others. In fact, Christianity, viewed accurately, should make us immensely humble. I couldn't save myself. God reached down to do it.

Pontius Pilate had a different answer to the question of why Jesus had to die. Interestingly, he asked that very question. He examined Jesus twice, and found him guilty of nothing. "I find no basis for a charge against him," he said (John 19:4). He was convinced by the crowd, including the religious leaders of the day, that Jesus should be crucified. Pilate thought Jesus had to die to maintain civil order in Jerusalem.

Why did the religious leaders want Jesus crucified? We looked at this briefly in Chapter 8. Jesus claimed to be the Son of God, the Messiah. The religious leaders thought this was blasphemy and tried to stone him (John 10:33). They didn't succeed on that occasion, but ultimately, on the eve of Passover, they got a second chance. The book of Matthew tells us that on the night of his arrest, Jesus was brought before the Sanhedrin, the religious ruling council. He was asked if he was the Messiah, the Son of God. Jesus affirmed that he was. "Then the high priest tore his clothes and said, 'He has spoken blasphemy! Why do we need any more witnesses? Look, now you have heard the blasphemy'" (Matthew 26:65). From the perspective of the religious leaders, Jesus was crucified because he claimed to be God in the flesh.

What I find interesting about these two perspectives is that they ring true. Pilate didn't want a riot. There was a crowd in town for Passover, threatening trouble. He correctly perceived that killing Jesus would pacify the crowd, and that's all he really cared about. The religious leaders heard Jesus say that he was God. If he wasn't, then the blasphemy charge was true and Jesus deserved death under Jewish law. All three "why's" intersected on that fateful Good Friday.

But here's the thing: the Romans didn't kill Jesus and neither did the Jews. I did.

Okay, the Romans did kill him, but not in the "why" sense – same with the Jewish religious leaders. They were involved, and they behaved badly, but they were tools.[84] Jesus was <u>destined</u> to die. He could have done a thousand things to avoid it. He went <u>voluntarily</u> to his death because he needed to go there. "Greater love has no one than this: to lay down one's life for one's friends," he said (John 15:13). That's what he did; he laid his life down. He took a bullet. Why? To pay for sin.

Whose sin? Mine. My sin made it necessary that he die.

I find it reassuring that the death of Jesus was part of God's plan. I like the fact that the majestic God of the universe initiated a solution to my brokenness, that he came to earth as an embryo, that he suffered and died for me, and that I don't have to try to earn my way to heaven. It proves that God is loving and forgiving. The Jesus I see dying on the cross is consistent with the Jesus I see giving the Sermon on the Mount, touching lepers, and washing people's feet. The "why" of the crucifixion shows how the pieces of evidence fit together seamlessly.

Why Did Jesus Rise From The Dead?

If you're with me so far, it probably makes sense that Jesus had to die. His death was the fulfillment of his mission; the payment for sin. It might be less clear why the resurrection occurred. Jesus said "it is finished" as he was expiring on the cross (John 19:30). Does the resurrection tell us that the crucifixion was not, in fact, the finish line?

I confess that I didn't understand this at first. I found myself as a young Christian having to explain Easter to other people. "Jesus rose from the dead," I said. "Okay, why?" "Umm ...."

Why did Jesus rise from the dead? What did it prove?

The resurrection proves the truth of Jesus's claims about himself. He said he was the Son of God. Jesus was "declared with power to be the Son of God by his resurrection from the dead" (Romans 1:4). If he is God, he had to rise. He had power over nature and the grave.

If the resurrection happened, it also means that there is hope for us to live after we die. "[T]he one who raised the Lord

Jesus from the dead will also raise us" (2 Corinthians 4:14). It proves the existence and the power of God. If God doesn't exist, or can't raise the dead, then there is no hope for us.

The resurrection was necessary in order to ignite the Christian church. It turned the cowering disciples into evangelists and it turned the skeptics Thomas and James into pillars of the church. It made believers out of commoners throughout the Middle East, and ultimately out of emperors and kings worldwide.

The resurrection is a "crowning" miracle. Jesus performed several miracles himself; he even raised a couple of people from the dead. But the resurrection of Jesus is the ultimate one. It's no coincidence that the crucifixion and resurrection occurred on Passover weekend. Passover celebrates the time when Moses led his people out of slavery in Egypt. Moses performed a series of ten miracles in front of Pharaoh. Only the tenth miracle got Pharaoh's attention (the one where his son died), and even that didn't last. Pharaoh let Moses lead the people out, but he soon had second thoughts and went after them. Then the crowning miracle occurred: the parting of the Red Sea. It was the final miracle in a series – the one still celebrated more than 3,000 years later every Passover. It secured the Exodus and gave the people a memorable milestone to inspire them in later years.

The parallels between the two "deliverance" miracles are fairly obvious. The parting of the Red Sea brought ultimate victory to God's people over Egypt. The resurrection brought ultimate victory to God's people over death. We, like Jesus, will see life beyond the grave.

I like the Friday-Sunday aspect of Christianity. The death of Jesus appeared to be a tragic defeat. But Sunday was just around the corner. This pattern gives us hope when we struggle in life. Friday is rough, but Sunday is coming.

Why isn't the evidence overwhelming?

As discussed in Chapter 9, Jesus appeared to more than 500 people after his resurrection, some of them skeptics. There is substantial evidence for the resurrection, but the case isn't airtight. Why not? God could have done it differently. Jesus could have appeared to emperors and kings all over the world to prove his resurrection. The events occurred in a corner of the world at a time without the Internet or mass media. God could have saved this miracle for 2016, when it would have been caught on somebody's smartphone. It would have gotten a billion hits on YouTube.

I have personally struggled with these questions. There is enough evidence to convince me, but if it were even stronger, more people would be convinced. Why is there this much room for doubt – why is there any room at all?

I'll tell you what I've concluded, and it's pretty stark: God intended for there to be doubt. He could have created a world without doubt. He could have created robots who did his bidding and didn't complain. But I believe that a central aspect of humanity is free will – the freedom to choose. God can always overwhelm that freedom, but He doesn't. He leaves room for doubt so people can choose. He leaves room for faith.

Ah, faith. What is faith? Faith and doubt go hand in hand. Doubt fills every corner of our world, from the jury room to the doctor's office. We have to manage our doubt and figure out how to act in the face of it. Making a decision and taking action in the presence of doubt requires faith. You exercise faith every time you step on an airplane. Most people have no idea how airplanes seemingly defy gravity – they trust the scientists.

A safe flight requires many competent actions by the pilot – we trust pilots even though most accidents involve pilot error. We trust the systems on board, the weather forecasters, the pilots of other planes, and the air traffic controllers. We're not in control and there's a statistical chance we'll crash. We step on board in faith.

Leaving room for some level of doubt means leaving room for faith. Why did God set up a system where faith on our part is required? The answer is that God wants a close relationship with us. God loves us so much that He desires more than just a casual relationship. Thus, He has designed a way for us to be part of the most intimate of relationships known to man – He made it possible for us to be part of His <u>family</u>. "For you are all sons of God through faith in Christ Jesus" (Galatians 3:26). God wants us to truly love Him like family members love each other.

Faith is the gateway to the relationship God desires. He doesn't force us to love Him. We can choose to love Him, or we can choose not to. There are consequences of each choice. But true love cannot be forced. It requires a choice. Faith is the exercise of that choice.

I don't want to pretend that I fully understand what "love" means. No one does. But here's an analogy: I made a choice to initiate a relationship with my wife, I made a choice to marry her, and she made the same choices (fortunately). Getting married is a step of faith. Nobody made us do it; we stepped out in faith because we loved each other. Love and genuine choice go together. The same is true for our love of God. Choice is a necessary element, and taking away the choice would defeat the purpose. The love wouldn't be real.

Don't get me wrong, I think the evidence for Jesus is very strong. The room for doubt is not gaping. People who honestly weigh the evidence with an open mind should conclude that the essential facts are true, including the resurrection. The problem for most people isn't that they find that the evidence supports one of the alternative theories, it's that they simply haven't looked at the evidence at all. God said, through the Old Testament prophet Jeremiah, "You will seek me and find me when you seek me with all your heart" (Jeremiah 29:13).

One of the great mathematical minds in history, Blaise Pascal, described this in a way that makes sense to me:

> Willing to appear openly to those who seek Him with all their heart, and to be hidden from those who flee from Him with all their heart, He so regulates the knowledge of Himself that He has given signs of Himself, visible to those who seek Him, and not to those who seek Him not. There is enough light for those who only desire to see, and enough obscurity for those who have a contrary disposition.[85]

The evidence is there for those who have eyes to see. But there is room for doubt. I acknowledge it. The existence of doubt has a logical explanation. It's consistent with how the world works.

12

DOES IT HOLD WATER?

Lawyers don't just gather all the evidence and dump it on a table for the jury to sort through. They sift and weigh the evidence, tossing out the chaff along the way. Just as important, they evaluate how the pieces of evidence relate to each other – how they fit. They put the pieces together into a coherent story. The "story" theory of trial practice has gained wide acceptance. Bare facts are unconvincing. What convinces jurors is when the facts make a compelling story that fits with the jurors' views of the world.

The point is, your evidence has to tell a story that makes sense. If your story doesn't fit the evidence, or requires logical disconnects, it probably isn't true. The expression "holding water" is common among trial lawyers and novelists. It means that the elements flow readily from one to another, are consistent with each other, and make sense together. There are no holes or cracks. The expression actually comes from the Bible, Jeremiah 2:13: "My people have committed two sins: They have forsaken me, the spring of living water, and have dug their own cisterns, broken cisterns that cannot hold water." The sole purpose of a cistern is to hold water, so if it's cracked, broken, or full of holes, it's useless. Let's see if the stories we've been looking at "hold water."

The best place to start is with the resurrection, because of the competing theories. Which one fits the evidence best?

Here's a summary:

Does The Theory Explain The Evidence?

	Physical Resurrection	Intentional Deception Theories			Grand Mistake Theories			
		Disciples Stole Body	Arose "In Spirit"	Later Invention	Mass Hallucination	Swoon	3d Party Stole Body	Went to Wrong Tomb
Empty Grave	✓	✓				✓	✓	✓
No Dead Body	✓	*					*	*
Appearances, Touching, Eating	✓				**	✓		
Skeptics Converted	✓							
Explosive Growth of Christianity	✓							
Sunday Worship	✓							
Belief held in face of torture, execution	✓				**			

* *Stolen body and wrong tomb theories explain absence of dead body in only one location.*

** *Hallucination may explain "appearances," though poorly; it does not explain touching or eating.*

It is readily apparent from this summary that none of the alternative resurrection theories comes close to holding water. They don't fit the evidence and they require leaps of logic. The "story" doesn't make sense. There are holes and cracks.

The theory that best fits the evidence, by far, is that an actual, physical resurrection occurred as described in the Bible. Of course, that theory only makes sense if God exists and material things are not all there is to reality. I believe those are the choices here: believe in God and the supernatural (miracles) or believe in a materialistic theory that defies facts and logic.

Let's pivot now and look at the totality of the evidence concerning Jesus. We'll review the essential points and the corroborating evidence from archaeology, non-Christian writings, and early Christian writings. For ease of reference, this is in tabular form:

Summary of Corroborating Evidence

	Essential Point Concerning Jesus	Biblical Evidence	Corroborating Evidence				
			Archaeology	Roman Writings	Jewish Writings	Skeptics' Writings	Christian Writings
1	Real person	✓	✓	✓	✓	✓	✓
2	Jewish ancestry	✓			✓	✓	✓
3	Virgin birth ("illegitimate")	✓			✓	✓	✓
4	From Nazareth	✓	✓		✓		✓
5	Forerunner – John the Baptist	✓			✓		✓
6	Great Teacher	✓		✓	✓	✓	✓
7	Disciples	✓			✓	✓	✓
8	Miracles	✓			✓	✓	✓
9	Called the Christ	✓		✓	✓	✓	✓
10	Rejected	✓			✓		✓
11	Condemned	✓	✓	✓	✓	✓	✓
12	Crucified	✓	✓	✓	✓	✓	✓
13	Resurrected (empty grave)	✓	✓		✓		✓
14	New Movement	✓		✓	✓	✓	✓
15	Persecution of followers	✓		✓	✓		✓

What this table shows is that on every essential point concerning Jesus, there is at least some corroborating evidence from outside the Bible. While the Bible is the main evidence, it is far from the only evidence. Nor does any of the extra-Biblical evidence <u>contradict</u> the Biblical evidence on any point of fact, though some of the non-Christian writers came to different conclusions about the facts.

The bottom line is that there is significant evidence concerning the birth, life, death, and resurrection of Jesus both inside and outside the Bible. The evidence holds water. It's a strong case.

13

WHAT SMART PEOPLE DO WITH EVIDENCE

Imagine going to the doctor, filling out all the forms, submitting to a thorough physical examination, having your blood tested and your blood pressure taken. The doctor looks in your ears, listens to your heart through a stethoscope, takes x-rays, and examines them in a light box. After all that, the doctor says "all done!" What's your reaction? Mine would be, "Well? What's the diagnosis?"

We don't examine evidence just for fun. Evidence is a means to an end, not an endpoint unto itself. When I present evidence to a judge or jury, there's a verdict at the end. There's no point in presenting the evidence unless it's leading to a decision. Consequences flow from the decision. The same is true here. The evidence about Jesus is there for all to see, and we all have to decide. Consequences will flow.

I'm going to close this book with examples of two types of people who did something with the evidence: skeptics and people who are experts at analyzing evidence.

Turnarounds of Skeptics

One of the amusingly false stereotypes of Christianity is that its adherents lack intelligence, that they're backwards, uneducated, or unenlightened. I demur! Actually, I don't take it personally. The people who think that are stupid. ;o)

Seriously, some of the smartest people who ever walked the planet <u>wrote</u> the Bible. I will pit the intelligence, reasoning ability, and writing talent of Luke and Paul against any of today's scholars. And some of the smartest people who ever lived started as skeptics and became Christians after examining the evidence.

I've already mentioned two skeptics. First was the famed Scottish archaeologist, **Sir William Ramsay**. He believed that the third gospel was written by someone other than Luke, sometime in the second century AD. He set out to prove it. His archaeological discoveries instead convinced him that "Luke's history is unsurpassed in respect of its trustworthiness." That's what we call a "180." If Ramsay had done that on the witness stand, the case would have ended right there. The other was **Ravi Zacharias**, born and raised in India, an atheist until the age of 17 when he survived a suicide attempt. He left his hospital bed promising to "leave no stone unturned in my pursuit of truth," and became a Christian.[86]

C.S. Lewis was a distinguished professor at both Cambridge and Oxford, and one of the greatest authors of the last century. He wrote *The Chronicles of Narnia* (a series that includes *The Lion, The Witch, and the Wardrobe*), *The Screwtape Letters*, and *Mere Christianity*. Lewis was a committed atheist until the age of 30. A classmate described him as a "riotously amusing atheist." As a young adult, he wrote to longtime friend Arthur Greeves, "I believe in no religion. There is absolutely no proof for any of them, and from a philosophical standpoint Christianity is not even the best." In the rarified air of Oxford, among colleagues like J.R.R. Tolkien (author of the *Lord of the Rings* books), Lewis examined the evidence and became convinced, describing himself as the most "dejected and reluctant convert" in all of England. He wasn't looking for God, and the revelation about God's existence was something of a fright to him. He became one of the leading spokesmen for Christianity in the 20th Century. Lewis, you may remember from Chapter 7, coined the "Lord, Liar, or Lunatic" options for the identity of Jesus (logically excluding the notion that Jesus was merely a good teacher).[87]

Lee Strobel is an award-winning journalist who made his mark at the *Chicago Tribune*. He was educated in both journalism and law (at Yale Law School). An avowed atheist in his late twenties, Strobel's world changed when his wife became a follower of Jesus. "I was an atheist for most of my life. I thought that the idea of an all powerful, all loving God was just silly." He viewed his wife's announcement as "the worst possible thing that could happen to our marriage."[88]

Strobel decided to use his training in law and journalism to investigate the credibility of Christianity. "I would do what I did at the Chicago Tribune. I would check out stories to see if they were true, if they could be printed in the papers. So I would investigate. I went out, and I applied those skills to the question of, 'Who is Jesus Christ?' I didn't do it with an antagonist attitude; I did it with a journalist's attitude . . . I said, 'Give me the facts. I'm going to look at both sides, I'm going to look at other world religions.'"[89]

Strobel investigated for almost two years, looking at evidence inside and outside the Bible. He found 110 facts outside the Bible recorded in ancient history that confirmed the Bible. "To maintain my atheism," he concluded, "I would have had to defy the evidence. To become a Christian, I just had to make a step of faith in the same direction that the evidence was pointing. That's logical, that's rational, and that's what I did."[90] Lee Strobel has written several books about the evidence, including the classic *The Case for Christ: A Journalist's Personal Investigation of the Evidence for Jesus*.

Dr. Francis Collins is one of the most eminent scientists alive today. He obtained his PhD in Physical Chemistry from Yale and his MD from the University of North Carolina. He was a distinguished Professor in internal medicine and human genetics at the University of Michigan and then became the Director of the Human Genome Research Institute in 1993 – what some would call the most prestigious job in science. The successful mapping of the human genome under his watch is one of the greatest scientific accomplishments of the last 50 years. Today, he is the Director of the National Institutes of Health.

Collins describes himself as a "rather obnoxious atheist" in his youth. "I think you wouldn't have enjoyed having lunch with me when I was in that phase. My mission then was to ferret out this squishy thinking on the part of people around me and try to point out to them that they really ought to get over all of that emotional stuff and face up to the fact that there really wasn't anything except what you could measure." While in medical school, he felt compelled to find out more about what it was that he had rejected. So with an intention of "shooting this all down," he went to speak to a Methodist minister. At the minister's suggestion, he read *Mere Christianity* by C.S. Lewis. He was surprised that someone of Lewis's intellect and accomplishments believed in Jesus. "Until then," Collins says, "I don't think anyone had ever suggested to me that faith was a conclusion that one could arrive at on the basis of rational thought."[91]

Collins examined the evidence and to his surprise, it made sense. The truth of the resurrection "was the most appropriate choice when presented with the data, [and] that was a new concept." Collins became a reluctant believer. "I didn't want this conclusion. I was very happy with the idea that God didn't exist." When the human genome project was completed and presented to the public by Collins and the President of the United States, Collins said, "It is humbling for me, and awe-inspiring to realize that we have caught the first glimpse of our own instruction book, previously known only to God."[92] Collins advocates rapprochement between faith and science, believing both to be true, rational, and consistent with each other.[93]

Simon Greenleaf was one of the greatest lawyers who ever lived. He was the Royall Professor of Law at Harvard University and author of what was known for many years as the authoritative text on the law of evidence. Greenleaf started out his examination of the resurrection believing that it was a "myth" or a "hoax." After thoroughly examining the evidence, he came to the exact opposite conclusion: "it was impossible that the apostles could have persisted in affirming the truths they had narrated, had not Jesus Christ actually risen from the dead." Greenleaf concluded that under the rules of evidence, the resurrection of Jesus was one of the best supported events in all of history.[94]

Those are six extremely smart people from various walks of life, highly accomplished in their fields. They're just the tip of the iceberg. The point is that highly intelligent and talented people, examining the evidence for Jesus, have concluded that the Biblical accounts are true. Even many diehard atheists have turned 180s after examining the evidence.

Expert Opinions

In addition to Simon Greenleaf, numerous lawyers and judges over the years have opined on the evidence concerning Jesus. Here are some statements from people whose expertise, like mine, is in the field of analyzing and weighing evidence:

Sir Edward Clarke, one of the most prominent barristers (trial lawyers) in British history, said, "As a lawyer, I have made a prolonged study of the evidences for the events of the first Easter day. To me, the evidence is conclusive, and over and over again in the High Court, I have secured the verdict on evidence not nearly so compelling. Inference follows on evidence, and a truthful witness is always artless and disdains effect. As a lawyer, I accept the gospel evidence unreservedly as the testimony of truthful men to facts that they were able to substantiate."[95]

Lord Charles John Darling was a Queen's Bench Justice in England. He said, "There exists such overwhelming evidence, positive and negative, factual and circumstantial, that no intelligent jury in the world could fail to bring in a verdict that the resurrection story is true."[96] Lord Darling is said to have given this statement at a dinner party,[97] and I think there's some hyperbole in it. But I agree with him that there is substantial evidence both positive and negative, factual and circumstantial.

John Warwick Montgomery earned eleven degrees in law, philosophy, theology, library science, and other fields. He has written over 125 scholarly journal articles and 40 books. He is an international human rights lawyer and distinguished professor who also made a name for himself debating prominent atheists. He was a "garden variety 20th century pagan" when he was challenged to examine the evidence concerning Jesus. Montgomery says, "The great miracle of the Resurrection may be a hard metaphysical pill to swallow, but swallow we can and must when the facts require it. Eliminate the factually impossible, and 'whatever remains, however improbable, must be the truth.'"[98] By "factually impossible," he's referring to the alternative resurrection theories. You can see Montgomery's lecture, *A Lawyer's Defence of Christianity*, on YouTube.[99]

Dr. J. N. D. Anderson was a scholar of international repute, one of the world's leading authorities on Islamic law, and Professor of Oriental Law at the University of London. He said "The empty tomb, then, forms a veritable rock on which all rationalistic theories of the resurrection dash themselves in vain."[100] Anderson found the evidence compelling: "it can be asserted with confidence that men and women disbelieve the Easter story not because of the evidence but in spite of it."[101]

Gordon Pearce is a regular lawyer, like me, but he's now retired. He didn't sit on a high court or teach at a prestigious university, he just practiced law. At age 20, he was an atheist; at age 30, he was a "comfortable agnostic." In his forties, while practicing law, he began to examine the evidence concerning Jesus, particularly the resurrection. He spent <u>seven years</u> doing it. He hadn't realized that "Jesus could be studied empirically as an historical figure." After concluding his investigation, Pearce wrote *From Skeptic to Christian: Persuaded by the Evidence*. His message: "The historical truth of the gospel accounts is supported by a rational evaluation of the evidence."[102]

This list, too, could go on and on. Many eminent lawyers through the centuries who have examined the evidence have come to the same conclusion I did. Lawyers are skeptics. They're used to examining both sides. They can smell lies. They've spent their lives sifting, sorting and analyzing evidence. They're evidence experts, like me.

This brings us back full circle to my story. I told you at the beginning of this book that I started as a skeptic, began examining the evidence at age 19, and haven't stopped examining it 40 years later. I owe it to you to tell you what I found influential, and what I have personally done with the evidence.

In the book of Matthew, I read that Jesus spoke to a storm and calmed it. The folks with him were amazed, and said,

"What manner of man is this, that even the winds and the sea obey Him!" (Matthew 8:27, King James Version). I too would have been amazed if I'd been there. I too would have asked, "What manner of man is this?" I was asking it as I continued reading the book of Matthew. Jesus was a different manner of man than I had ever seen. It was as if a light bulb blinked on.

I continued reading the Bible for several months, and then reading some additional material about the resurrection, which fascinated me. I loved the fact that the evidence was physical as well as literary, that people like Thomas had insisted on touching the wounds. I just could not give credence to the alternatives. I felt it would require greater faith to disbelieve than to believe.

I made a decision to follow Jesus. I didn't wait 40 years to do it, when all the evidence was in and the questions all answered. It was just a few months after reading the book of Matthew. I had examined enough evidence to be convinced. I was convinced that Jesus was not just "a man" but the Son of God, that he had died for my sins and risen from the dead, and that I would follow him. Today, I have studied reams of additional evidence and it has only solidified my convictions.

Looking back, I must tell you that although I was skeptical, I was also curious. I had an open mind. I dug for the evidence I was interested in. I believe this was critical to the path I took.

Every person's journey is different. You may come to a different conclusion. You may take more time, or less time. The things you drill down on, that interest you, may be different from what interested me. I'll give you one piece of advice, though: maintain a bit of skepticism. Don't fall for weak arguments. Don't take any wooden nickels.[103]

Conclusion

There is, in my opinion, a rational basis for believing in the virgin birth, miracles, death, and resurrection of Jesus. There is plenty of evidence to support all of these things. Believing them is reasonable. It holds water.

I'd be the last person to overstate the case. It's not a "slam dunk." It's not "airtight." I've never seen a case where there wasn't room for doubt. That room exists here.

I hope this examination of the evidence about Jesus has been worthwhile for you, no matter where you end up. In my view, there is no more interesting thing to talk about, no search that is more meaningful. Wherever you are in the process, I hope you will keep at it.

RESOURCES FOR FURTHER STUDY

1. Strobel, L: *The Case For Christ: A Journalist's Personal Investigation of the Evidence for Jesus* (Grand Rapids: Zondervan, 1998).

2. Lapide, P: *The Resurrection of Jesus: A Jewish Perspective* (Minneapolis: Augsburg Publishing House, 1983).

3. Habermas, G and Licona, M: *The Case for the Resurrection of Jesus* (Grand Rapids, MI: Kregel, 2004).

4. McDowell, J: *New Evidence That Demands A Verdict* (Nashville: Thomas Nelson, 1999).

5. Bruce, FF: *The New Testament Documents: Are They Reliable?* (Downer's Grove: Inter Varsity Press, 1981, first edition 1943).

6. Yancey, P: *The Jesus I Never Knew* (Grand Rapids: Zondervan, 1995).

7. Keller, T: *The Reason For God: Belief in an Age of Skepticism* (New York: Penguin Books, 2008).

8. Zacharias, R: *Can Man Live Without God?* (Nashville: W Publishing Group, 1994).

9. Lewis, CS: *Mere Christianity* (New York: HarperOne, 2015, first edition 1952).

Acknowledgments

I acknowledge that I am a sinner, saved by grace. To me, this is an important acknowledgement in a book of this type. I've read others that portray a "holier-than-thou" attitude, some from both sides of the argument. My approach is that I'm a flawed person who has traveled a rocky path. I wish to provide guidance to those just starting down the path.

The "grace" that has been generously provided to me includes the help of many people. I had some wonderful professors in college (UCLA) who taught me to "think like an engineer," and more in law school (Michigan) who taught me to "think like a lawyer." I've forgotten almost every fact I was taught. But I carry with me today the ability to separate wheat from chaff and to build something meaningful out of solid bricks (and to mix metaphors!). I have had some wonderful mentors and colleagues in my law career who have shone some light on my path.

I have dedicated this book, as I dedicated my novel (*The Underwater Window*), to my wife, Tracey. At this writing, we've been married 37 years and counting, and we are partners in every sense of the word. She reads every draft of everything I write, and she's an excellent editor of both style and substance. In Chapter 1, I mentioned that when I got to college, I met some people who were "markedly different;" their faith made a difference in their everyday lives. Tracey was one of those people. I owe her not only for guiding the writing of this book, but for starting me down the path 40 years ago.

This book was truly 40 years in the making. I started gathering evidence from the beginning. After a while, I started teaching what I was learning. The book has been refined by the feedback of my students in Sunday School and Bible study classes over the years. I'd like to call out the senior high students at Grace Bible Church in Ann Arbor, Michigan for being among the first and best of my critical reviewers. I found it impossible to pull any wool over their eyes.

Besides being a student of extra-Biblical evidence, I could not have written this book without gaining a pretty deep knowledge of the Bible. That has been a 40-year process as well. I firmly believe that the Bible is an amazing book, but that you must know it well to use it properly. I credit some influential Bible teachers and pastors, and spiritual mentors like Dr. Bruce Fong of Dallas Theological Seminary. I have received some excellent teaching from professors at DTS, and someday I hope to have a degree from that place. I also admire the training provided by Bible Study Fellowship International, which I observe on a daily basis as Tracey leads a large BSF class in Pasadena.

Several people read the manuscript and provided helpful input: Tracey Stephenson, Matthew John, Jim and Linda Fletcher.

I have received inspiration from several sources. I admire the writings of C.S. Lewis, Philip Yancey, Lee Strobel, Ravi Zacharias and Josh McDowell. Matthew John motivated, encouraged, and asked me to write. Britt Hemphill, my old college teammate and current ministry colleague, deserves a special shout because without him, I wouldn't have the "it works" stories (missionary training center, Dinangat, Nairobi slums) of Chapter 10.

An endless supply of grace continues to come from my Heavenly Father, who guided this book in subtle and obvious ways. I won't claim "inspiration" in the sense of Scripture, but I gratefully acknowledge both His gentle nudges and two-by-fours to the head.

NOTES

(Endnotes)

1. Richard, Larry, "Herding Cats: The Lawyer Personality Revealed," (Atlanta: The Remsen Group, 2002), p. 4.

2. Federal Rule of Evidence 401.

3. This story is recounted in detail in chapter 17 of *From the Trenches: Strategies and Tips from 21 of the Nation's Top Trial Lawyers*, Worden, John, ed. (Chicago: ABA Publishing, 2015), pp. 247-268.

4. Bruce, FF, *The New Testament Documents: Are They Reliable?*, (Downer's Grove, Ill.: Inter Varsity Press 1981), ch. 7.

5. Ramsay, William M, *The Bearing of Recent Discovery on the Trustworthiness of the New Testament* (London: Hodder & Stoughton, 1915), p. 222.

6. McRay, John, interview quoted in Lee Strobel, *The Case for the Resurrection: A First-Century Investigative Reporter Probes History's Pivotal Event* (Grand Rapids: Zondervan, 2010).

7. Bruce, *The New Testament Documents*, ch. 7.

8. Papias of Hierapolis, in Eusebius, *Ecclesiastical History*, Book 2, Chapter 15. Papias was the bishop of Hierapolis, and lived from roughly 60 to 130 AD. He wrote a five volume work entitled "Interpretation of the Oracles of the Lord" which no longer exists, but is widely referenced by other authors. See "Is Mark's Gospel an Early Memoir of the Apostle Peter?," by J. Warner Wallace, in *Cold-Case Christianity*, Jan. 17, 2014, http://coldcasechristianity.com/2014/is-marks-gospel-an-early-memoir-of-the-apostle-peter/.

9. There are other creeds or hymns recorded in the New Testament, for example in Philippians chapter 2 and First Timothy chapter 3.

10. Von Campenhausen, H, "The Events of Easter and the Empty Tomb," in *Tradition and Life in the Church* (Philadelphia: Fortress, 1968), p. 44.

11. Habermas, Gary, quoted in Lee Strobel, *The Case for Christ: A Journalist's Personal Investigation of the Evidence for Jesus* (Grand Rapids: Zondervan, 1998), pp. 314-15.

12. "Religion Among the Millenials," Pew Research Center, February 17, 2010, http://www.pewforum.org/2010/02/17/religion-among-the-millennials/.

13. Chesterton was called a "colossal genius" by George Bernard Shaw, another genius. "Orthodoxologist," *Time*, 11 October 1943.

14. Chesterton, GK, "The Twelve Men," in *Tremendous Trifles* (London: Methuen & Co., 1909), p. 68.

15. There are some who claim that evolution disproves the notion of a creator. This is a fascinating discussion, and I follow this debate closely. For present purposes, the important point is that evolution and creation are not necessarily mutually exclusive. There are some folks at the extreme ends of the spectrum of this debate who say that they are mutually exclusive, but the majority of people (myself included) believe that both evolution and creation occurred. The spectrum between the extremes is filled by various views as to how <u>much</u> evolution has occurred. Because <u>any</u> involvement of a creator disproves atheism, the essential question is whether God was involved <u>at all</u> in the origin of the universe and life. Debating whether evolution occurred in "macro" or "micro" amounts is interesting, but not critical to the question of God's existence.

16. Louis Pasteur lived in France from 1822 to 1895. He won the Distinguished Cross and the Grand Cordon of the French

Legion of Honor. He invented the process that bears his name – pasteurization – by which food is sterilized and kept safe for consumption. He solved a French silkworm epidemic. He discovered and implemented the process of vaccination to prevent diseases. He found cures or successful vaccinations for rabies, anthrax and diptheria. He founded the famed Pasteur Institut, which today is a leader in AIDS research, among other things. Pasteur's work served as the springboard for such diverse branches of science and medicine as microbiology, bacteriology, stereochemistry, virology, immunology and molecular biology.

17. Vallery-Radot, René, *The Life of Pasteur* (New York: McLure, Phillips & Co., 1902), p. 142.

18. Crick, Francis and Orgel, LB, "Directed Panspermia," *Icarus*, 19:341-46 (1973).

19. Denton, Michael, *Evolution – A Theory in Crisis* (Bethesda, Md.: Adler and Adler, 1986). Denton is a molecular biologist and medical doctor.

20. Penzias, Arno, quoted in Malcolm W. Browne, "Clues to Universe Origin Expected," *New York Times*, March 12, 1978, p. 54.

21. Ross, Hugh, *The Fingerprint of God: Recent Scientific Discoveries Reveal the Unmistakable Identity of the Creator* (New Kensington, Pa.: Whitaker House, 2000).

22. Collins, Francis, quoted in Steven Swinford, "'I've Found God' Says Man Who Cracked Genome," *The Sunday Times*, Nov. 6, 2006, http://rense.com/general71/found.htm.

23. Kistiakowsky, V, quoted in *Cosmos, Bios, Theos: Scientists Reflect on Science, God, and the Origins of the Universe, Life, and Homo Sapiens* (Chicago: Open Court, 1992), p. 51.

24. Denton, Michael, *Nature's Destiny: How the Laws of Biology Reveal Purpose in the Universe* (New York: The Free Press, 1998), p. 372.

25. Lear, J, *Aristotle: The Desire to Understand* (Cambridge: Cambridge University Press, 1988), pp. 248-49.

26. In his book *River Out Of Eden*, prominent atheist Richard Dawkins writes that the universe has "no design, no purpose, no evil and no good, nothing but blind, pitiless indifference." Further, "you won't find any rhyme or reason in it, nor any justice." Dawkins, R: *River Out of Eden: A Darwinian View of Life* (New York: Basic Books, 1995), p. 133.

27. "Martin Luther King, Jr. – Acceptance Speech," at NobelPrize.org, https://www.nobelprize.org/nobel_prizes/peace/laureates/1964/king-acceptance_en.html.

28. Bernstein, Leonard, *The Joy of Music* (Pompton Plains, NJ: Amadeus Press, 2004), p. 29. Bernstein wrote that "[n]o matter what rationalists we may profess to be, we are stopped cold at the border of this mystic area. It is not too much to say *mystic* or even *magic*: no art lover can be an agnostic when the chips are down. If you love music, you are a believer, however dialectically you try to wriggle out of it" (pp. 11-12).

29. Kavanaugh, Patrick, *The Spiritual Lives of Great Composers* (Nashville: Sparrow Press, 1992), pp. 35-42.

30. 30 Yancey, Philip, *Rumors of Another World: What on Earth Are We Missing?* (Grand Rapids: Zondervan, 2003), p. 37.

31. The writers were: Matthew, Mark, Luke, John, Peter, Paul, James and Jude. There is no consensus as to who authored the Epistle to the Hebrews, although it might have been Paul.

32. Tacitus, Publius Cornelius, *Annals of Imperial Rome*, 15:44.

33. Josephus, Flavius, *Antiquities of the Jews* (93-94 A.D.), Book 20, chapter 9.

34. Ibid., Book 18, chapter 3.

35. "Jesus Christ (Non-Christian sources)," *Encyclopedia Britannica Online*.

36. King, Larry, quoted in Ravi Zacharias, *Jesus Among Other Gods* (Nashville: Thomas Nelson, 2002), p. 38.

37. Quran, chapter 19. On receiving the announcement that she will bear a "holy child" (19:19), Mary says "How shall I have a son, seeing that no man has touched me, and I am not unchaste?" (19:20).

38. Klausner, Joseph, *Jesus of Nazareth* (New York: The Macmillan Company, 1925).

39. Celsus, quoted in Origen, in H. Chadwick, *Origen: Contra Celsum*, (CUP 1965), p xxviii.

40. Yancey, Philip, *The Jesus I Never Knew* (Grand Rapids: Zondervan, 1995), p. 32.

41. Dostoyevsky, Fyodor, quoted in Lee R. McGlone, *The Minister's Manual* (San Francisco: Jossey-Bass, 2011), p. 390.

42. Josephus, Flavius, *Antiquities of the Jews* (93-94 A.D.), Book 20, chapter 9.

43. Ibid., Book 18, chapter 5.

44. *Contra Celsum*, Ibid. n. 39, p. xxviii.

45. "Mara Bar-Serapion," in *Early Christian Writings*, http://www.earlychristianwritings.com/text/mara.html.

46. "The First Epistle of Clement to the Corinthians," *The Lost Books of the Bible*, accessed April 15, 2016, http://www.sacred-texts.com/bib/lbob/lbob15.htm.

47. "House from Jesus' time excavated," (December 23, 2009) in *Israel 21c: Uncovering Israel*, accessed April 15, 2016, http://www.israel21c.org/house-from-jesus-time-excavated/.

48. Korb, Scott, *Life in Year One: What the World Was Like in First-Century Palestine* (New York: Riverhead Books, 2010), p. 109.

49. Durant, Will, *Christ and Caesar, The Story of Civilization* (New York: Simon & Schuster, 1972), p. 557.

50. Ibid.

51. Baxter, J Sidlow, *Explore the Book* (Grand Rapids: Zondervan, 1987), p. 308.

52. Lewis, CS, *Mere Christianity* (New York: MacMillan, 1952), p. 56.

53. "Mara Bar-Serapion," Ibid. n. 45.

54. Tzaferis, Vassilios, "Crucifixion – the Archaeological Evidence," *Biblical Archaeology Review* Jan/Feb 1985, pp. 44-53.

55. For a brief and relatively balanced review of the scientific pros and cons, see Viviano, Frank, "Why Shroud of Turin's Secrets Continue to Elude Science," *National Geographic* April 17, 2015.

56. Updike, John, *A Prayer for Owen Meany* (New York: Harper Reprint, 2012).

57. In November 1990, twelve ossuaries (bone boxes) were discovered in a burial cave in south Jerusalem. Two featured the name "Caiaphas." One of the boxes with the name "Caiaphas" was ornately decorated, as befitting a person of high rank. Zvi Greenhut, "Burial Cave of the Caiaphas Family," *Biblical Archaeology Review*, BAR 18:05, Sep/Oct 1992.

58. Some authors have spun fanciful tales about what they think may have happened to Jesus's body. An author in the 1990s suggested that Jesus's body is buried in southern France. Conveniently, the "body" is under numerous feet of rock in

a place where excavation is unfeasible. This is a far cry from producing Jesus's dead body. Paul Schellenberger and Richard Andrews, *The Tomb of God: The Body of Jesus and the Solution to a 2000-year-old Mystery* (New York: Little Brown, 1996). In 2007, a moviemaker claimed to have discovered Jesus's bones in an ossuary in Jerusalem. He generated a lot of publicity, hoping to capitalize on this find. His claim, however, was easily and thoroughly debunked, and the fanfare lasted only a day or two. "The Lost Tomb of Jesus," Discovery Channel, March 4, 2007; see also Simcha Jacobovici and Charles Pellegrino, *The Jesus Family Tomb* (New York: Harper Collins, 2007).

59. Bruce, FF, *The New Testament Documents*, Ibid. n. 4, ch. 9.

60. Pliny the Younger, *Letters* 10.96-97.

61. Lapide, Pinchas, *The Resurrection of Jesus: A Jewish Perspective* (Minneapolis: Augsburg Publishing House, 1983), p. 117.

62. Moule, CFD, *The Phenomenon of the New Testament* (London: SCM Press, 2012), p. 3.

63. For example, Luke's gospel says that three women discovered the empty tomb: Mary the mother of Jesus, Joanna (Salome), and Mary Magdalene. John's gospel only mentions Mary Magdalene. However, it was common for ancient writers to omit details they did not think important. The mention of one person does not preclude the presence of others. John did not think it critical to name all of the women, and Luke did. This, again, is actually corroborative because it shows that the four gospel writers had different perspectives, and were not simply writing an agreed-upon story.

64. Lapide, *The Resurrection of Jesus: A Jewish Perspective*, p. 95.

65. Arnold, Thomas, *Christian Life, Its Hopes, Its Fears, and Its Close*, 6th ed. (London: T. Fellowes, 1859), pp. 15-16.

66. Peter is the one disciple who ever exhibited any boldness, but he wavered back and forth. He denied Jesus three times during the night after Jesus was arrested, and the realization left him in a puddle of tears. He was not present at the scene of the crucifixion. Interestingly, he became the chief spokesman for the church, as recorded in the book of Acts, shortly after the resurrection. He died a martyr for his faith. His later boldness is actually evidence <u>for</u> the resurrection. His discovery of the empty tomb, and seeing the risen Jesus, gave him the boldness to preach the facts he had witnessed. Knowing Peter, he would not have been capable of preaching lies boldly.

67. Colson, Charles, *Loving God* (Grand Rapids: Zondervan, 1983), pp. 68-69.

68. Ibid.

69. Craig, William Lane, quoted in Strobel, Lee, *The Case for Christ* (Grand Rapids: Zondervan, 1998), p. 285: "nobody espouses that [stolen body] theory today." See also Frank Morison, *Who Moved the Stone?*, p.88 (Grand Rapids: Zondervan, 1958): "So far as I know, there is not a single writer whose work is of critical value today who holds that there is even a case for discussion."

70. Collins, G, personal communication with Gary Habermas, 21 February 1977, quoted in Gary Habermas, "Explaining Away Jesus' Resurrection: Hallucination," *Christian Research Journal*, Vol. 23 / No. 4 (2001), http://www.equip.org/article/explaining-away-jesus-resurrection-hallucination/.

71. Johnson, Luke Timothy, *The Real Jesus* (San Francisco: HarperOne, 1996), p. 30.

72. Metherell, Alexander MD, quoted in Strobel, Lee, *The Case for Christ* (Grand Rapids: Zondervan, 1998), p. 262.

73. Ibid, p. 265.

74. Edwards, Dr. William E et al, "On the Physical Death of Jesus Christ," *Journal of the American Medical Association*, Vol 255, No. 11, March 21, 1986, pp. 1455-63.

75. Metherell, quoted in *The Case for Christ*, p. 270.

76. Craig, William Lane, *Reasonable Faith: Christian Truth and Apologetics* (Wheaton, Ill.: Crossway Books, 3d ed. 2008), p. 377.

77. These are the only serious theories. Even more fanciful theories spring up from time to time. William Lane Craig debated a college professor who proposed that the empty tomb and resurrection appearances could be explained by an "identical twin brother who was separated from [Jesus] at birth, and who showed up in Jerusalem at the time of the crucifixion, stole Jesus's body, and then showed himself to the disciples." William Lane Craig, "The Evidence for Christianity," http://www.bethinking.org/is-christianity-true/the-evidence-for-christianity. Dr. Craig says "I think this example is instructive because it shows to what desperate lengths the skeptic has to go to avoid the resurrection of Jesus."

78. I have quoted Lapide a few times, so I had better say who he is (or was; he died in 1997). He was an Orthodox Jew, a rabbi, a Pharisee who believed in God and the possibility of resurrection. He was a Jewish New Testament theologian, a soldier in the Jewish regiment of the British Army during World War II, and a diplomat for the state of Israel. After examining the evidence, he concluded that Jesus was raised from the dead physically. Lapide did not believe that Jesus was the King Messiah promised by the Old Testament.

79. Lapide, *The Resurrection of Jesus: A Jewish Perspective*, p. 126.

80. Craig, WL, "Jesus' Resurrection," http://www.reasonablefaith.org/jesus-resurrection.

81. Lincoln said this to his brother-in-law, Ninian Edwards, according to Edwards. James Reed, "The Religious Sentiments of Abraham Lincoln," *Scribner's Monthly*, July 1873, p. 336, cited in "Abraham Lincoln: The Old School Presbyterian Convert," http://www.leben.us/volume-9-volume-9-issue-3/365-abraham-lincoln, accessed November 26, 2016. See also "The Preachers: James Smith (1807-1874), *Mr. Lincoln and Friends*, http://www.mrlincolnandfriends.org/the-preachers/james-smith/, accessed November 26, 2016.

82. King, ML, Jr., "For All . . . A Non-Segregated Society," A Message for Race Relations Sunday, drafted Sept. 4, 1956 and delivered Feb. 10, 1957, in The Martin Luther King, Jr. Papers Project of Stanford University, https://swap.stanford.edu/20141218225500/http://mlk-kpp01.stanford.edu/primarydocuments/Vol4/10-Feb-1957_NonSegregatedSociety.pdf.

83. King, ML, Jr., *Letter From a Birmingham Jail* (1963).

84. I find statements that Jewish people are "Christ killers" to be ludicrous. The "real killers" (to borrow a phrase from O.J. Simpson), are those of us throughout history who have committed sin; we are the ones who created the need for Jesus to go to the cross. Call me a Christ killer – I deserve it. The Romans carried out the execution, but nobody thinks of calling modern-day Italians "Christ killers." Only a relatively small number of Jewish people (religious leaders) participated in the decision to have Jesus executed by the Romans, and to suggest that any other Jews, including present-day Jews, were among the "killers" is illogical. The charge that people making "Christ killer" statements are prejudiced is a fair one. By the same token, any claim that the Bible is "anti-Semitic," because it discusses the part played by some Jewish people, is also unfair.

85. Pascal, Blaise: *Pensees* (Trotter Transl.) (Public Domain, 1660), http://www.ccel.org/ccel/pascal/pensees.txt, accessed May 6, 2016.

86. Zacharias, Ravi, *Walking From East to West: God in the Shadows* (Grand Rapids: Zondervan, 2006).

87. Lewis, CS, *Surprised By Joy* (New York: Harcourt Brace, 1955); Downing, David: *The Most Reluctant Convert: C.S. Lewis's Journey to Faith* (InterVarsity Press 2002).

88. Strobel, Lee, quoted in "Another Special Life in Christ," https://poptop.hypermart.net/testls.html; see also Lee Strobel, *The Case for Christ*, pp. 15-16.

89. "Another Special Life in Christ," Ibid.

90. Ibid.

91. "Other Voices: Francis Collins," http://www.pbs.org/wgbh/questionofgod/voices/collins.html.

92. Simon, Stephanie, "Faithful to God, Science," Los Angeles Times. http://articles.latimes.com/2006/aug/17/nation/na-collins17/3]

93. See Collins, F, *The Language of God: A Scientist Presents Evidence for Belief* (Free Press 2007).

94. Greenleaf, Simon, *An Examination of the Testimony of the Four Evangelists by the Rules of Evidence Administered in the Courts of Justice* (London: A. Maxwell & Son, 1847), p.29.

95. Clarke, Edward, quoted in John Stott, *Basic Christianity* (London: InterVarsity Fellowship, 1969), p. 47.

96. Darling, Charles John, quoted in Michael Green, *Man Alive!* (Chicago, IL: InterVarsity Christian Fellowship, 1969), p. 54.

97. McDowell, Josh, *New Evidence that Demands a Verdict* (Nashville: Thomas Nelson, 1999), p. 219.

98. Montgomery, John Warwick, *The search for ultimates: a Sherlockian inquiry*, Christian Legal Journal (Spring 1993), reprinted in John Warwick Montgomery, *The Transcendent Holmes*, (Ashcroft,

British Columbia: Calabash Press, 2000), 119-135. The internal quotation by Montgomery is from the fictional character Sherlock Holmes, in A.C. Doyle, *The sign of the four, the complete Sherlock Holmes*, Vol. 1 (Garden City, New York: Doubleday, 1930), p. 111.

99. John Warwick Montgomery, *A Lawyer's Defense of Christianity*, Village Lutheran Lectures on Christianity and Culture, https://www.youtube.com/watch?v=hxMEisHKewc.

100. Anderson, JND, *The Evidence for the Resurrection* (London: Inter-Varsity Press, 1950).

101. Anderson, JND, *Christianity: The Witness of History* (London: Tyndale Press, 1970), p. 90.

102. Pearce, Gordon, *From Skeptic to Christian: Persuaded by the Evidence* (Enumclaw, WA: WinePress Publishing, 2002), pp. xi-15.

103. The expression "don't take any wooden nickels" arose in the early 1900s. It means "stay alert to fraud." Linguists believe it gained a footing during the Depression, when naïve country folk came to the big city, susceptible to being fooled by swindlers. A wooden nickel is fake and worthless. My personal view is that the alternative resurrection theories are wooden nickels.

FACT OR FICTION?

This Book is part of 'The Mosaic Course'

The Mosaic Course is an introductory course in World Religions, exploring the uniqueness and significance of Jesus Christ from the perspectives of different religious traditions and worldview assumptions.

www.themosaiccourse.org

Made in the USA
Monee, IL
16 November 2021